A History
of the
North Carolina
Third Mounted
Infantry Volunteers

U★S★A★

March 1864 to August 1865

By Ron V. Killian

HERITAGE BOOKS
2008

HERITAGE BOOKS

AN IMPRINT OF HERITAGE BOOKS, INC.

Books, CDs, and more—Worldwide

For our listing of thousands of titles see our website
at
www.HeritageBooks.com

Published 2008 by
HERITAGE BOOKS, INC.
Publishing Division
100 Railroad Ave. #104
Westminster, Maryland 21157

International Standard Book Numbers
Paperbound: 978-0-7884-1605-7
Clothbound: 978-0-7884-7512-2

CONTENTS

INTRODUCTION

The writing of this history was a labor of love. Many years of research and attempts to understand exactly which event occurred, in relation to other events, consumed many hours. An attempt was made to actually see the battlefields, where possible. Some of the areas are too remote and not really accessible without professional guides. These areas, as a rule, were not visited. Additionally, some of the actual battlefield locations are not known. They have become part of the local folklore and legend. We have only near approximations, as to their actual location.

The battles, engagements, skirmishes, and other military events included in this work, are **only** those which can be verified by the *War of the Rebellion* records, or some other primary source, or the secondary sources of notable authorities, such as Vernon Crow, Dr. Noel Fisher, and Dr. Richard Current, and Dr. John Barrett, to mention a few of the authorities in the mountain theater of the Civil War. Isolated and unsubstantiated events, "Grandpa said," and other such materials, while very interesting and often true, are not included in this work. To many people, this will be interpreted negatively, and viewed with considerable adversity. This style of writing also complicates events that actually occurred so that one might wonder, "what did occur? "An effort was made to avoid additional complications.

Endnotes are used, as opposed to footnotes, to allow the reader to refer to a source if desired, while not disrupting concentration. An effort was made to use several sources in many of the endnotes. This was done to allow any reader who might desire, to review the thoughts of various historians on a particular event.

While objectivity was a coveted goal in this work, an attempt was made to dispel the long held view that Colonel George Kirk was some sort of mountain iniquitous evil from Tennessee, who came to destroy Western North Carolina. Granted, the Third Mounted Infantry effectuated some awesome deeds. Some of these were totally unnecessary and carried out with malice. Yet, one must remember, war is death and destruction- pure and simple! Colonel Kirk and the Third Mounted Infantry were duly sworn volunteer soldiers, Federal troops, **not renegades, or Bushwhackers,** as they were frequently called. Without doubt, the Biblical verse applies: "let him without sin cast the first stone." There are no halo polishing saints in war. Colonel Kirk was no exception. Neither should he be regarded as any worse than the Confederate Army operating in the Western Carolinas and Eastern Tennessee. It has been stated many times that the Civil War was a war of brother against brother, family against family. In the mountains of Western North Carolina and Eastern Tennessee, these words could not have been more completely authentic and genuine.

FORMATION OF THE NC THIRD MOUNTED INFANATRY

During the American Civil War, loyalty was sharply divided in the mountain regions of North Carolina and Tennessee. This division became so replete, that east Tennessee considered forming a separate state.[i] Sentiment in western North Carolina was less intense, yet significant enough to compel many to join the Union Army or, in some cases, to simply, "Hide." This variance led to the formation of a number of Union Army military regiments in North Carolina from the years 1862 through 1863[ii]

This work is concerned with the formation and eventual history of the Third Mounted Infantry Regiment of Volunteers of North Carolina, usually referred to as the North Carolina Third Mounted Infantry. The Third Mounted Infantry was plenary with men who opposed secession from the Union, slavery, as well as many of the other objectives of the Confederacy. The price for this devotion to the Union would be high. These soldiers were often referred to as Lincoln's Loyalists, "Tories," bushwhackers, "home Yankees," and a great assortment of other uncomplimentary terms.[iii]

The Third Mounted Infantry was authorized on February 13, 1864, by General John Schofield, Department of the Ohio. General Schofield stated in Special Order No. 44:

> Authority is hereby granted to Major G.W. Kirk, of the Second North Carolina Mounted Infantry, to raise a regiment of troops in the eastern front of Tennessee and western part of North Carolina. The regiment will be organized as infantry and will be mustered into the service of the United States to serve for three years, unless sooner discharged. The regiment will rendezvous as soon as practicable at headquarters Department of the Ohio, or other place to be to be hereinafter designed, to be mustered into service. The commanding officer is authorized to mount his regiment, or such portion of it as may from time to time be necessary, upon private or captured horses. This regiment will be known as the Third Regiment of North Carolina Mounted Infantry. By command of Major-General Schofield.[iv]

The Third Mounted Infantry would ultimately enlist over 850 soldiers. The ages of these men ranged from age 16, the youngest, to 48, the oldest. The median age of the soldiers in this regiment falls between late teens to early thirties.[v]

All fourteen of North Carolina's mountain counties are represented in the regiment. Dr. Ina W. van Noppen states in her book, *Stoneman's Last Raid*, that Yancey county gave 79 men, and Madison county 60 men to the Third Mounted Regiment. These numbers are based on the 1890 census of Union Army soldiers and their spouses.[vi] A degree of caution must be applied to this statement. Many of these men gave fraudulent background information when they enlisted, as well as to the 1890 Census clerks. The logic of this action is simple: they feared retribution from their Confederate friends and neighbors.

Tennessee supplied a substantial number of men to the Third Mounted Infantry. At any rate, the enlistment of the soldiers occurred in Tennessee. The same caution must apply to this lot of soldiers. They may have given incorrect information in an attempt to shield themselves from contempt and violence from their friends and neighbors back home. Ten counties in Tennessee were the primary enlistment area for soldiers joining the Third Mounted Infantry. As one would expect, these counties border the mountain counties of North Carolina. The countries are: Carter, Cocke, Grainger, Greene, Jefferson, Johnson, Knox, Polk, Sevier, and Washington.[vii]

As stated previously, the Third Mounted Infantry was authorized in February of 1864. An examination of the various companies reveals much as to the strength of the regiment at any given time. Companies A, B, C, D, and E rosters convey the fact that about half the regiment enlisted between March and October of 1864. This would be the soldiers who took part in the early exploits and skirmishes of the regiment. Company F enlistment period is June to December of 1864. Of course, these dates and times are not absolute. There are exceptions. Company H was formed between November of 1864 until about April 1865. As a point of interest, a great number of these men enlisted at Knoxville. Company I evince a nearly total 1865 enlistment. In addition, many of these men also enlisted at Knoxville. Company K (there is no Company J) is the unique company of the regiment. All the private soldiers enlisted at Burnsville, North Carolina. All enlisted in March of 1865. These men served about six months.[viii]

It was most intriguing to see that the regiment had a number of musicians. In some cases the instruments were named: fife, drum, and bugle. There seems to have been at least ten musicians. No mention was made as to the type of music rendered.[ix]

Other support staff mentioned were: teamsters, wagoners, cooks, and surgeons. No mention was made of chaplains. None were identified by

2

name. One can but hope that these valiant men had access to clerics of some description.[x]

The NC Third Mounted Infantry recorded thirty-nine deaths due to both battle injury and disease. This is approximately 4.5% of the total fighting force. Other deaths may likely have occurred and were not noted on the mustering out records. However, this percentage is comparable to other Civil War regiments of the same size. For example, the One Hundred and Twenty First Pennsylvania Infantry had a fighting force of 891 soldiers. This is very near the size of the Third Mounted Infantry. The 121st recorded sixty-six deaths due to all causes. This is about 7.3% of the total fighting force. This unit fought at Gettysburg, Chancellorsville, Spotsylvania, Petersburg and Five Forks, to mention but a few of their battle engagements. [xi] It seems evident that the Third Mounted Infantry was a fighting regiment.

The Third Mounted Infantry had seventy-eight desertion charges. This is about 9.1% of the total fighting force. The desertions do not seem to have followed any pattern, as to age, enlistment area, rank, or any other criteria. The regiment issued one Dishonorable Discharge. As any military person knows, this is an extreme action which borderlines a curse to most military personnel.[xii]

The Regiment experienced five enemy captures. Again, these follow no pattern or fall under any criteria. Those captured were both young and not so young. They all seem to be honorable men. Again, it is a certainty that captures occurred which are not recorded on any regimental records.

It is perhaps noteworthy to mention that in every company one is able to ascertain father and son, brother and brother, cousins, men with the same surname, evidence that enlistment was a family commitment. This is even more notable in light of fact that this has been a tradition in America since the Revolution. In the American Civil War, family commitment seems more prevalent than in some of the other wars of the nation.

Each of the companies had unique qualities. Company D seems to have had the largest number of native Americans from, perhaps, the Cherokee Nation. An analysis of the names of soldiers in Company D tends to bear out this fact. Company F had the largest number of desertions, Company A had the fewest numbers of desertions. Company H had the largest number of causalities, Company A, the smallest.

At first glance, the Third Mounted Infantry appears to be a very typical Civil War military regiment. The fact is, however, this regiment is very atypical. An entire company enlisting in the same month and year, from the same small town is not typical. Native Americans fighting with the

United States against other native Americans fighting with the Confederacy is most unusual. The most unconventional and confounding aspect about the Third Mounted Infantry is the fact that its members were Southern mountain men at war with other Southern mountain men.

CAMP VANCE RAID: JUNE 13 - July 15, 1864

The raid from Morristown, TN into Burke County, NC was the first **major** military operation of the NC Third Mounted Infantry. As has been stated previously, the regiment was authorized by General John Schofield on February 13, 1864. Colonel Kirk did not officially join the regiment until March 14, 1864.[xiii] At this point in the development of the regiment, segments of Companies A, B, C, and D comprised the mainstay of the military strength of the regiment.

The regiment left Morristown, TN on June 13, 1864. There is disagreement as to the number of troops on this raid. Some sources state the number was 130. Other sources give 300 men present on the raid.[xiv] A dispassionate figure is probably somewhere between these two views. A force of 130 seems too small. A force of 300 may have exceeded the actual number of combat ready troops who were members of the regiment in the late Spring of 1864.

Upon leaving Morristown, under orders from General Schofield, the regiment marched through Bulls Gap, into Greeneville, TN, and entered Carter County on June 25.[xv] At this point, Colonel Kirk enlisted the services of a noted and knowledgeable guide, John V. Franklin.[xvi] Franklin was from Linville Falls, NC and was a close childhood friend of Keith Blalock, the famous Federal spy. The regiment crossed Big Hump Mountain, went up the Toe River, and passed the Cranberry Iron works.[xvii] The regiment camped near the house of David Ellis. On the 26 of June, they passed Pinola and crossed the Linville River.[xviii] On the 27 of June, Franklin led the raiders down the east side of the mountains and through Mitchell County, NC. The unit passed through the county undetected. About sundown of June 27, the regiment reached Upper Creek, 12 miles from Morganton, NC. Prudence would have dictated that the unit camp for the night and resume the operation the next day. Colonel Kirk, the 'daredevil' that he was, ordered the men into the water and pushed on toward Camp Vance.[xix]

Camp Vance was located about six miles from Morganton at Berry's Pond, near the railhead. The camp was named for the governor of North Carolina and was used for conscript instruction. It was felt that the camp might be a hindrance on the return trip to East Tennessee. Therefore, it had to be captured. The camp contained about 250 young conscripts. The regiment arrived at the door of the camp on the evening of June 27.[xx]

Colonel Kirk had two major objectives for this raid. The first was to push on to Salisbury, NC and free the Federal prisoners at the Salisbury prison camp. A second objective was the destruction of the Yadkin river bridge. For these purposes, Kirk had included a locomotive engineer from Tennessee on the raid. He hoped to capture a locomotive at the Morganton railhead, and load rail cars with troops for the trip to Salisbury. Of course, all of this was contingent upon the capture of Camp Vance. Morganton was at least 80 miles behind Confederate lines. The temerity of this raid is absolutely awesome.[xxi] As was stated by John P. Arthur in, *The History of Watauga County,* "Kirk's raid revolutionized matters in the mountains. The confederates had no means to stop an incursion into the Piedmont from Tennessee, which could cut off the major railroad from the Carolinas to Richmond."[xxii]

Colonel Kirk was not aware that the conscripts were unarmed. Lieutenant William Bullock was the commander of the conscripts. He had decided that the men would be armed on the 28 of June. Major McClean, the camp commandant, was not present on the morning of the 28th. Colonel Kirk came out of the woods with a flag of truce. Kirk went to the camp's headquarters and demanded immediate surrender. Little resistance was given. Nevertheless, ten conscripts and one officer were killed. The regiment then proceeded to burn down the camp, except for the hospital. Colonel Kirk took 132 prisoners and 48 horses and mules on the return march to East Tennessee.[xxiii]

One might wonder, where was the Confederate army during this two week "blitzkrieg" from Tennessee? There seems to have been some confusion as to who had jurisdiction. Colonel J.B. Palmer, commander of the Western District of North Carolina states, "I have no cavalry under my command. ...on his return to Tennessee he plundered and burned my residence in Mitchell county. He committed no other depredations in my district, though he committed many, I understand, east of the Blue Ridge."[xxiv] This report was addressed to General Cooper, Adjutant General, in Richmond. Correspondences between Colonel Melton, Assistant Adjutant General, and Major J.B. Hoge, suggest that the Adjutant General's office thought that Colonel Palmer had been replaced by General James Martin. It was decided that General Martin was responsible.[xxv]

As Colonel Kirk left the Morganton area, a small force of Home Guard from Burke, Caldwell, Catawba, and Iredell counties attempted an interception. Kirk used 20-25 of the captive prisoners as a shield. He is quoted as having said, "Look at the damned fools, shooting their own

6

men."[xxvi] According to William Trotter in his book, *Bushwhackers: The Civil War in North Carolina, The Mountains,* one prisoner named Bowles, was killed by the Home Guard.[xxvii] In addition, Kirk was wounded by the Home Guard during the engagement at Brown's Mountain.[xxviii]

The Regiment left the main road at Israel Beck's farm and traveled along the west side of Brown's Mountain. They re-entered the main road on Jonas Ridge. Colonel Allen Brown, commanding the 1st Regiment of North Carolina Troops, overtook the Third Mounted Infantry about 20 miles from Morganton, at a place known as Winding Stairs. This area is located near the now abandoned Piedmont Springs resort, about 21 miles from Morganton. The Winding Stairs are actually a narrow path on top of Jonas Ridge. The Third Mounted Infantry held a superior position, and with about 20 to 30 soldiers cut the Confederates to ribbons. Kirk's forces had Spencer rifles and, along with the choice position, the outcome was never in doubt.[xxix]

In addition to wrecking Camp Vance, Kirk took 250 prisoners, and as previously stated, was able to return to Knoxville with 132 of the prisoners. He destroyed the Morganton Railroad depot, recruited 40 men for his command, in addition to the acquisition of a large amount of food stuffs.[xxx] The Third Mounted Infantry suffered about seven causalities, the Confederates about twelve to fifteen, including Colonel Avery, commander of the Morganton troops.[xxxi]

Colonel Kirk and the Third Mounted Infantry received glowing praise from the Union high command. General John Schofield sent Colonel Kirk(then a Captain) a letter of praise on July 24 from Atlanta:

Captain: I have received...a report of your operations in the recent expedition into North Carolina, and take pleasure in conveying to you the assurances of Major-General Sherman of his appreciation of the services you have rendered our cause, to which I add my own thanks to you, and through you to the officers and men of your command, for the gallant and successful manner in which you have conducted the expedition. Such daring and hazardous expeditions should be undertaken but rarely. You can, in general, render more effective service by organizing the element in North Carolina hostile to Jeff Davis into a series of scouting companies....[xxxii]

General Sherman responded with an additional letter of praise for Colonel Kirk and the Third Mounted Infantry. In addition, General Sherman also stressed that Colonel Kirk should refrain from undertaking additional hazardous expeditions and instead, concentrate on organization of new companies in the Western Carolinas.[xxxiii]

Views on the Camp Vance raid are not universally laudatory for the Third Mounted Infantry. Noel Fisher, in his work, *War at Every Door: Partisan Politics & Guerrilla Violence in East Tennessee 1860-1869,* states that "Kirk's first operation, an attempt to disrupt the railroad between Salisbury and Greensboro, was a fiasco." [xxxiv] Kirk's efforts are likened to other raiders from Tennessee, such as Colonel William Clift.[xxxv] This view seems unjustifiable in light of the effect it seems to have had on the Confederate army. An example is found in a letter from Colonel Palmer, who, on December 10, 1864, is bemoaning the fact that he has moved his command to East Tennessee from Western North Carolina. This move was per instructions from General Lee. He states that he must deal with Colonel Kirk and the Third Mounted Infantry.[xxxvi] As stated early by John Arthur, Kirk's raid changed things in the mountains. This fact alone, made the Camp Vance raid worthwhile to the Union cause in the North Carolina-Tennessee area.

ACTION AT MORRISTOWN AND THE SKIRMISH
AT RUSSELVILLE, TENNESSEE AND BEYOND
October 28, 1864- December 7, 1864

On October 18, 1864, Captain J. Dick Bushong CSA, reported to General Breckinridge that the strength of the Union forces assembled near Bulls Gap were as follows: Eighth Tennessee Cavalry, 800; Eighth and Ninth Tennessee Infantry, consolidated strength 200; Thirteenth Tennessee Cavalry, 400; Third North Carolina Scouts (Kirk), 400; one battery of heavy artillery (Kentucky); 100-days men, 150.[xxxvii] A sizable military force was about to be unleashed on the Confederate forces in eastern Tennessee.

On October 27, 1864, General John C. Vaughn states in his account of the Morristown and Russellville altercation: "had a skirmish yesterday and today, in which my troops were successful, driving the enemy. So far they have shown no disposition to advance."[xxxviii] Colonel John B. Palmer, Fifty-eighth NC Infantry, commanding the Mountain District of North Carolina relays, in a dispatch to General Breckinridge, "On the 27th of October, I proceeded ...to Morristown for the purpose of conferring with General Vaughn, whose forces I found skirmishing the enemy.[xxxix] On the 28th, Colonel Palmer's forces were ordered to Russellville by General Vaughn. Colonel Palmer states: "I selected a line about one mile in advance of Russellville, on the Morristown road, and was moving my command into position when General Vaughn's staff officer arrived from the front and requested me form my line in rear of Russellville."[xl] At this point, things get a little murky, as to what actually occurred. Colonel Palmer goes on to state: " ... General Vaughn's retreating Cavalry swept by my men in the wildest disorder."[xli] Colonel Palmer states that his command was small because most of his troops were in Bulls Gap at General Vaughn's command. He also stresses that his mountain howitzer was loaned to General Vaughn's Cavalry and captured by the enemy.[xlii]

General Vaughn's version of the action at Morristown is somewhat different. He states: "I regret to say that my command was stampeded at Morristown this morning. I lost four pieces of artillery. My command is now formed at this place in order. The enemy is in check....I lost a good many men in prisoners."[xliii]

The Union version of this action is a little more enlightening. Due to the failure of General Hood to capture Chattanooga and hold lower East Tennessee, General John Williams' cavalry division was ordered to Georgia from East Tennessee, by way of Paint Mountain, Tennessee, and Asheville, North Carolina. Upon receipt of this information, General Alvan Gillem moved his forces, of which the Third Mounted Infantry was a part, against General John Vaughn's cavalry. In his report, General Gillem gives credit to the three Tennessee cavalry regiments, with special praise for Lieutenant Colonel Ingerton, of the Tennessee Thirteenth Cavalry. The Third Mounted Infantry was not mentioned in Gillem's report. Yet, Colonel Kirk's regiment placed 400 plus troops in the action at Morristown and the skirmish at Russellville. General Gillem seems to have had a special dislike of Tennessee rebels. The action at Morristown was basically Tennessee Union forces against Tennessee rebel forces. This may explain Gillem's failure to mention the North Carolina Third Mounted Infantry's role in the action.[xliv]

In the written report of the battle, General Gillem gives an account of enemy weapons and supplies taken by his forces. He mentions that 300 small arms were taken. These were given to citizens of East Tennessee to be used against the guerrillas for protection of life and property.[xlv]

In conclusion, General Gillem mentions that Vaughn's command lost over 500 men in killed, wounded, and captured. General Vaughn was wounded in this action.[xlvi] Federal causalities were 18 wounded and 8 deaths.

General Vaughn lived much of his life in Roane County, Tennessee. He was not a professional military officer. He witnessed the Fort Sumter action first hand, having been in Charleston on business at the time. He was wounded at Martinsburg, West Virginia. After recovery, he was transferred to East Tennessee. He served with General Johnston's forces in North Carolina after the Army of Northern Virginia fell, and acted as part of the Jefferson Davis withdrawal forces when Davis fled Richmond. Vaughn's command seems to have been a very undisciplined element at times. He was not highly respected by other Confederate officers.[xlvii] Colonel Palmer's remarks are indicative of this lack of respect.

Information on the Third Mounted Infantry's role in this action is simply not in great supply. Neither the Union nor Confederate reports give any specific information. However, it is certain that whatever role the regiment was given, they carried out to the fullest. Nevertheless, without Dyer's *Compendium* we would probably not have verification of **any** involvement by the Third Mounted Infantry.[xlviii]

The Third Mounted Infantry was involved, in what appears to be, a continuation of the Morristown Action on November 5 and 6 of 1864.

Reports of this skirmish **do not exist** as part of the official military records. This skirmish proved to be a unique challenge **just to verify its existence.** Dyer's *Compendium* states that a skirmish occurred involving the Third Mounted Infantry on November 5 and 6, 1864.[xlix] The skirmish is listed as having taken place at Big Pigeon River, Kentucky. No official records exist in the *Army Records for the War of the Rebellion,* or the OR as it is commonly called. The records exist only as a surgeon's report in the National Archives Records. Doctor Marion Roberts, a surgeon with the Third Mounted Infantry, filed a medical casualty report. In this report Doctor Roberts states that Sergeant Leander Simmons of Company A, and Private James Eller of Company B sustained wounds in a skirmish **near the North Carolina border.** One must be cautious in any attempt to determine exactly in which state this skirmish occurred. The following situations are some of the possibilities concerning this battle.

As General Vaughn's forces attempted to move out of Tennessee to link with General Breckinridge, various skirmishes and military actions occurred. The Third Mounted Infantry was supporting General Gilliam's cavalry in Gillem's attempt to stop General Vaughn's advance. General Stoneman's Army also occupied Abington, Virginia on December 14, 1864. Stoneman's forces disrupted the hearing that was in progress for the deceased Confederate General John Hunt Morgan.[l] The Third mounted Infantry's Big Pigeon skirmish could have occurred in support of this operation. Any of these operations could have brought about the Third Mounted Infantry's skirmish at the Big Pigeon River. However, any scenarios about this battle are speculation. The skirmish could just as likely have occurred in the Sevierville, Tennessee area on the Pigeon River. All of these suggested possibilities are in the correct general geographic area. What is known about this skirmish exist only in Doctor Robert's Surgeon Report.[li] Unfortunately, it can only be concluded that a skirmish occurred and that it involved the Third Mounted Infantry.

On December 7, the Third Mounted Infantry was sent to Paint Rock, North Carolina via Sevierville, Tennessee. The regiment was to assist the Fourth Tennessee in holding the passes over the mountains into North Carolina until East Tennessee was evacuated by the enemy. When this was accomplished, the Third Mounted Infantry was to scour the mountains and clear them of any remaining rebels.[lii]

The major Confederate forces operating in this area were under the command of General Basil Duke, brother-in-law of the deceased General John Hunt Morgan. At this point, Colonel Richard Morgan, brother of

General John Hunt Morgan, was in command. General John Vaughn, from the Morristown and Russellville engagements, was attempting to move toward Wytheville and the lead-works. Attention was given to the order and priority of the attack schedule: attack Vaughn first, then the lead-works and salt-works later, or attack the salt-works and lead-works, and deal with Vaughn afterwards. It was decided to use the former alternative.[liii]

Considerable damage was done to the salt and lead works. Duke's command was badly beaten at Kingsport. Eighty-four prisoners were taken, among which was Colonel Richard Morgan, brother of General John Hunt Morgan. The city of Bristol was taken by General Burbridge, and also Abington, Virginia.[liv]

The Confederate account of this series of actions and skirmishes is somewhat different from the report given by Gillem and Burbridge. The commander of the North Carolina Mountain District, Colonel J.B. Palmer, states that the Third Mounted Infantry and the Fourth Kentucky occupied Paint Rock in Madison County, North Carolina. He states that the Third Mounted Infantry retreated when he advanced. A severe storm raised the waters so greatly that his forces could not cut off Colonel Kirk's escape. Palmer states that the Third Mounted Infantry had moved toward Greasy Cove in Washington County, Tennessee. It was suspected that Kirk's target was the Watauga and possibly, the Holston River bridge. Palmer states he forced Kirk to retreat toward Knoxville.[lv]

Colonel Palmer goes on to say that General Vaughn's retreat from south of Bulls Gap endangered his forces. It appears that Palmer felt he had to assist General Breckinridge, who was now in North Carolina. He states that his forces were to the maximum of expansion. Colonel Palmer seems to have sensed that the end was not far away. He seems to have been a very perceptive commander.[lvi] The Third Mounted Infantry was now positioned to assist with the largest, and the final, military operation in the mountains: Stoneman's Raid, in the Spring of 1865.

WAYNESVILLE, NORTH CAROLINA

Several months after the Morristown and Russellville skirmishes, on February 1, 1865, Colonel Kirk and the Third Mounted Infantry left Newport, Tennessee with 600 raiders for an attack on Waynesville, North Carolina. The regiment crossed the Smokies at Sterling Gap. They encountered little resistance. This was one of a number of forays on Waynesville made by Colonel Kirk and the Third Mounted Infantry.

The dates for Colonel Kirk's raid on Waynesville vary from February 1, to March 1, 1865. [lvii] The most agreed upon date seems to be February 4, 1865. The Third Mounted Infantry spent the better part of the day in Waynesville. This is a considerable period, taking into account that Waynesville was a mere village of twenty to thirty houses. Citizens were beaten, articles were stolen, especially jewelry and silver items. The home of Revolutionary War hero Colonel Robert Love was burned. No purpose was ever manifested for this action. The jail was opened. All prisoners fled to the countryside. The jail was then systemically destroyed. Some of the jail inmates eventually joined the Third Mounted Infantry. [lviii]

After the town had been totally wrecked, Kirk and the Third Mounted Infantry moved Southwest on the Balsam Gap Road. Their intent was to cross the mountains and camp for the night, about seven miles from Waynesville. After dark, a company of Haywood County militia and some very angry farmers made an attack on Kirk's position. After a blistering barrage from the Third Mounted Infantry's Spencer rifles, they withdrew. Meanwhile, Colonel Stringfield gather together about 300 men, of which many were Cherokees, to confront Kirk's regiment. A small sharp shooting company engaged Kirk before the main force arrived. Colonel Kirk realized his troops were "bushed" and chose not to charge, but rather to withdraw. On February 6, he passed through Balsam Gap. He moved past the village of Webster and on toward the Tuckaseegee River. He ran directly into Colonel Stringfield at Soco Gap with his 300 men. Soco Gap is on the Haywood-Jackson County line. It was the most important passage used by the Indians through the Balsam Mountains. A furious skirmish occurred. The Confederates ran low on ammunition. This was Colonel Kirk's saving grace. Again, he "pulled it out" and was able to escape back to Tennessee, by way of Indian Gap, which is on the Swain County, North Carolina-Sevier County, Tennessee line.

13

The Waynesville raid was more costly than usual. There were Union causalities and deaths, more than usual. The Confederates lost twenty men, twenty more were captured, and over 100 horses were stolen. All things considered, Waynesville was not such a bad exchange.[iix] The Regiment was not captured, which was a real possibility for a period of time. Kirk was lucky this time.

Kirk's Waynesville raid caused eyes to open in Richmond. It has been stated that Grant read the Richmond newspapers regularly. The raid, and Kirk's additional fame, impressed Grant greatly. The federal press declared that Kirk captured three Rebel flags, and killed more men than he captured. These feelings reinforced the view: Waynesville was not such a bad exchange after all.[lx]

STONEMAN'S RAID

Major General George Stoneman had a varied career in the Union army. Perhaps Stoneman's most significant and consequential position occurred under General Hooker. When General Hooker became commander of the Army of the Potomac, he reorganized the army. The cavalry was formed into a separate corps and General Stoneman was given the command. In July of 1863 Stoneman became Chief of the Washington Cavalry Bureau. The following winter(1864) he became the commander of the XXIII Corps, in the western army. In April, he was assigned to the Army of the Ohio. At this point, he was engaged in the Battle of Atlanta. He asked permission of General Sherman to extend his duties to liberate Union prisoners at Andersonville. This venture proved unsuccessful. General Stoneman was captured and remained a prisoner for several months.[lxi]

In February of 1865, Stoneman was given the command of the District of East Tennessee, still part of the Department of Ohio.[lxii] Stoneman's Raid was finalized on March 23, 1865, comprising nine cavalry regiments: 15th Pennsylvania; 10th and 11th Michigan; 12th Ohio; 8th, 9th, and 13th Tennessee; 11th and 12th Kentucky. The regiments were placed under the command of General Alvan Gillem [lxiii] The Raid was conducted to prevent an escape by the Army of Northern Virginia westward as Sherman and Grant forced Lee's surrender in the final stages of the war.

Plans were carefully made to avoid a rear attack on Stoneman's forces. When the raid commenced, General Davis Tillson, commander of the Fourth Division, Department of the Cumberland, was charged with the duty of following Stoneman, and occupying all mountain passes in Northwest North Carolina.[lxiv] General Tillson division was divided into two brigades: First Brigade, 2nd and 3rd *North Carolina Mounted Infantry,* 4th Tennessee, 1st Ohio Heavy Artillery, 1st U.S. Colored Heavy Artillery, Indiana Light Artillery; Second Brigade: 34th Kentucky, 1st Tennessee, 2nd Tennessee, 7th Tennessee Mounted Infantry, 2nd Ohio Heavy Artillery; Artillery: Ohio, Light, 21st Battery, Ohio Light, 22nd Battery, 1st Michigan Light, Battery I, First Michigan Light Battery M, 1st Illinois Light, Battery K, Illinois Light, Henshaw's Battery, 1st Tennessee Light, Battery B.[lxv] This was, indeed a formidable Force.

The total number of men involved was about 5,000. However, the number is not totally agreed upon by historians. Some sources give 6,000 as the number of cavalrymen.[lxvi] The newly formed Cavalry Division of the

District of East Tennessee rode out of Knoxville on Tuesday, March 21, 1865. On March 22, the Division concentrated at Mossy creek, Tennessee in readiness to invade western North Carolina. On March 24, Stoneman moved to Morristown. He detached the Third Brigade, under Colonel Miller to make a detour from Bulls Gap to the railroad at Jonesboro. This was done to cut off a military force thought to be in the rear of the Division.[lxvii]

General Davis Tillson gathered the forces of the First Brigade of his Infantry Division supporting General Stoneman on March 22, at Morristown, Tennessee. It was decided that the Second and Third North Carolina Mounted Infantry were needed, along with the Fourth Tennessee and the First U.S. Colored Heavy Artillery, to cover the mountain passes. By April 4, General Tillson's Division had reached Roan Creek, Tennessee. On April 5, the Fourth Tennessee and the First U.S. Colored Heavy Artillery moved to Taylorsville, Tennessee. The same day, Colonel Kirk moved with the Second and Third North Carolina Mounted Infantry toward Boone. On April 7, the Second North Carolina occupied Deep Gap, and Major Rollins of the Third Mounted Infantry, with 200 men, occupied Watauga Gap. Colonel Kirk with 406 men of the Third Mounted Infantry remained in Boone.[lxviii]

The role of the Third Mounted Infantry in the western North Carolina and southwestern Virginia raid of General Stoneman is second **only** to the Camp Vance raid in June of 1864. This important raid was designed to "end the war," much like General Sherman's raid. Stoneman was to destroy, not fight battles.[lxix] The Third Mounted Infantry played no small role in the outcome of this raid.

On March 28, General Gillem's Division reached the North Carolina line. General Stoneman sent Captain Koegh, his aide-de-camp, into Boone to dislodge any resistance. The Captain and the 12th Kentucky "fired at will." The end was never in doubt. When the conflict ended, 9 confederates were dead and 68 captured. In addition, the jail and most of its records were burned.[lxx]

Stoneman now moved toward Wilksboro, North Carolina. He split the command at this point. General Gillem took part of the force and moved near Lenoir, North Carolina, via Flat Gap Road. Gillem crossed the Blue Ridge at Blowing Rock and rejoined Stoneman at Wilksboro. Stoneman moved toward Wilksboro through Deep Gap. Gillem burned the large cotton factory, and destroyed the road above the town. In addition, he burned other supplies, destroyed bridges, and did considerable damage to the North Carolina Central, and the Danville and Greensboro railroads.[lxxi]

General Tillson had given the order for Colonel Kirk to march on Boone, April 3, 1865. Kirk, commanding both the Second and Third North Carolina Mounted Infantry, reached Boone on April 6. Boone, in 1865, can hardly be classified as anything more than a small village. It had less than 300 people. Watauga County had only about 5,000 people.[lxxii] Colonel Kirk was instructed to barricade the Meat Camp Road leading through State Gap and also to barricade another road not listed on the maps at Sampson Gap. Meat Camp was actually in Ashe County, North Carolina, north of Watauga County. The Meat Camp was one of the first places to be settled in the High Country area. It had been used as a packing house by hunters as early as 1799. The name was given to a nearby creek. From this creek, the road got its name. Presently, this road would tie in, in a very general fashion, with U.S. highways 221, 321, and 441.[xxiii]

Colonel Kirk was well acquainted with the unionist support, as were his men, in the Watauga area. He did not feel it was necessary to barricade all roads in the area. The Banner Elk road was such a road and was not barricaded. However, Colonel Kirk and the Third Mounted Infantry had a special dislike for Boone and Watauga County. An elderly man by the named of Price, two of his sons, and a nephew was arrested by the Home Guard. A confederate major led a mob who lynched the four outside Boone. The four were union sympathizers. [lxxiv]

Colonel Kirk made his headquarters at the same house used by General Stoneman during his brief stop at Boone. The conduct of the two men is reported to have been quite different. Stoneman was courteous to the owners. Colonel Kirk is reported to have been quite the opposite. His troops were very disorderly, leaving the house and grounds in filth and disrepair.[lxxv] Any military forces stationed in Watauga County had to more or less supply their own subsistence. Most of the local residences' homes were ransacked. All available food was taken. To combat this, the local people hid food, as well as anything else of value.

After barricading the roads, Colonel Kirk transposed the Watauga courthouse into a virtual fort by cutting holes in the walls and erecting timbers. As stated earlier, 200 of Colonel Kirk's men were at Watauga Gap. A fort was built there by setting timbers on end where the road crossed the mountain near Green Park. The timbers were obtained by wrecking a summer house of a Lenoir man. Word quickly spread that Colonel Kirk was in the area.[lxxvi] An attempt was made to gather forces from Salisbury and other areas by Major Avery, to carry out a raid on Kirk's camp at Blowing Rock. No troops were available.[lxxvii]

On April 3, General Stoneman was in Hillsville, Virginia. Little resistance was encountered from the local Confederate forces. . On April 6, the raiders were in Wytheville, Virginia. Again, little resistance was incurred. General Stoneman moved his forces in preparation to return to North Carolina on April 7. On April 8, the Division was in Martinsville, North Carolina. Confederate Colonel J. T. Wheeler attempted to stop the raiders. One Union soldier was killed and five were wounded. The Confederates lost about 20 horses and failed in their attempt to stop Stoneman's advance.[lxxviii]

Stoneman encountered resistance at Shallow Ford, and Mocksville. A skirmish occurred on April 11. On April 12, the Division reached the outskirts of Salisbury. A skirmish occurred at Grant's Ford. [lxxix] The bridge over Grant's Creek had to be repaired. Trains could be heard by General Stoneman's raiders leaving Salisbury on the South Carolina and Morganton railroads. General Stoneman directed that a detachment should cross the creek several miles above the bridge. This force would cut the railroads, capture the train, and get to the rear of the town and engage the enemy.[lxxx] Another detachment of troops, under the command of Lieutenant Colonel Smith, was ordered to cross the creek at a lower point. Upon engagement of the enemy by all the detachments, Colonel Miller's brigade was ordered to advance on the main road. Pursuit continued until the enemy was routed. Former Lieutenant General , now Colonel, John C. Pemberton's troops were in total disarray. About eighteen hundred prisoners were taken, along with eighteen artillery pieces and property worth immense amounts of money.[lxxxi] The railroad was destroyed as far north as a few miles from Lynchburg. The railroad south of Salisbury was in ruins for many miles. All property not destroyed was sent to East Tennessee, along with prisoners and artillery. General Stoneman's forces withdrew on April 13, and reached Lenoir on April 15.[lxxxii]

On April 15, General Stoneman turned over the command to General Gillem. Specific instructions were conveyed to Gillem as to what should be done with the Division. General Palmer was to go to Lincolnton and scout the Catawba River. General Brown was to go to Morganton, and later link with General Palmer. General Miller was to go to Asheville and clear a communications channel to Greeneville, Tennessee.[lxxxiii]

On May 4, the Third North Carolina Mounted Infantry was sent, by General Tillson, to Rabun Gap, by way of Waynesville and Franklin. Instructions were relayed to the Second and Third North Carolina Mounted Infantries, through Colonel Hawley, to move to Asheville at once. The

Second was to wait until the Third Mounted Infantry arrived. Upon Colonel Kirk's arrival with the Third Mounted Infantry, the Second Mounted Infantry would immediately move to Greeneville. Colonel Kirk was to remain several days in Asheville to collect stragglers of his, and other commands and then return to Greeneville.[lxxxiv]

Colonel Kirk arrived in Asheville on May 17. During this entire operation, there were no causalities in General Tillson's Division. The Division contained 4, 500 troops. As of May 18, 1865, the Third Mounted was still in Asheville.[lxxxv]

ASHEVILLE: WESTERN NORTH
CAROLINA CITADEL

Asheville was the foremost city in Western North Carolina, in terms of support for the Confederacy. The city had about 1,200 residents in 1865. By all accounts, it was a rough, frontier town, "A small country village." It lacked all of the basic amenities such as a water and sewer system, street lights, telegraph service, railroad service, a market, and a general connection with the outside world. However, it did have one very important facet: a factory making the best Enfield-pattern muskets in the Confederacy. For this reason, if for no other, it was an important city to the Confederate cause.[lxxxvi]

When General James Martin, the Commander of the District of Western North Carolina, learned that the Union cavalry was approaching Asheville, he immediately moved his entire command to the Swannanoa Gap. This is far less dramatic than it sounds. His command consisted of Palmer's brigade: the Sixty-second, the Sixty-fourth, and the Sixty-ninth regiments; a South Carolina battery; J.R. Love's regiment.[lxxxvii] General Martin's forces made it difficult for the Union cavalry, led by General Alvan Gillem, to reach Asheville. They cut down trees, rolled boulders in the road, and employed other such delaying tactics to block Gillem's way. General Gillem soon realized this was too much to deal with and simply headed forty miles to south via Rutherfordton, North Carolina. He reached Rutherfordton on the 21 of April. On the 22 of April, Gillem's forces passed Howard's Gap, in Polk County, and crossed the Blue Ridge. Gillem entered Hendersonville soon after dawn on the 23rd of April.[lxxxviii]

On April 24th, a formal meeting was held between Generals Gillem and Martin. An agreement was worked out by which the Union army would pass through Asheville on the way to Tennessee. The Confederate army would supply Gillem's cavalry nine thousand rations. On the 25 of April, the Union forces arrived in Asheville. The Generals dined together and General Gillem left Asheville that night on his way to Greeneville, Tennessee. His army remained in Asheville, but they departed the next day, April 26. At nightfall on the 26th of April, General S. B. Brown returned with a military force and ransacked the city.[lxxxix]

General Martin evacuated Asheville on April 29th, 1865. He moved his command to Waynesville, about 30 miles west of Asheville. Federal troops, under the command of General Davis Tillson, returned to, and occupied Asheville. General Stoneman directed General Tillson to send the

Second Mounted Infantry, commanded by Colonel Bartlett, from Greeneville, Tennessee into the mountains, south of Asheville. Colonel Kirk and the Third Mounted Infantry were ordered to leave Greeneville and go into the mountains north of Asheville. General Tillson arrived in Asheville on April 30. Kirk and Bartlett arrived on May 1, 1865.[xc] Colonel Kirk was sent to Rabun Gap, via Waynesville and Franklin, shortly after arrival in Asheville.

Asheville was under attack even before General Gillem and Colonel Kirk's operations occurred in late April . Colonel Isaac M. Kirby of the One Hundred and First Ohio Infantry, First Brigade, First Division, approached Asheville on April 3, 1865. Colonel Kirby left Lick Creek, Tennessee via the Greeneville and Asheville road to Paint Rock (Madison County, North Carolina). From Paint Rock, the brigade went to Warm Springs and bivouacked for the night of April 4. At this point, captured deserters informed Kirby that Asheville had a force of about 2,000 men and 20 guns. Six hundred men of Thomas' command were in the mountains near Waynesville, and there was also a small local force of 30 to 40 men. It was also learned that the enemy had heard rumors of Colonel Kirk and the Third Mounted Infantry's approach and had sent out a unit to meet him.[xci]

Colonel Kirby learned at Marshall (Madison County) that information concerning his brigade had already reached the Confederates at Asheville. In addition, the road from Burnsville had been blocked to dissuade Colonel Kirk's approach to Asheville. Kirby's brigade burned two bridges over the French Broad River four miles below Asheville.

Colonel Kirby had been instructed by General Stanley, Fourth Corps Commander, "Not to sacrifice the life of one man for the town of Asheville." To add even more confusion to Kirby's situation, a heavy storm was in progress. After consultation with his staff, Kirby decided that his force of 900 troops was inadequate to defeat General Martin's force with a strong, hard fight. A withdrawal of the brigade was ordered. Colonel Kirby reached his camp at Lick Creek in Tennessee on April 11, 1865.[xcii]

The "reign of terror" for the city of Asheville continued for the better part of a year. Citizens were accosted for having buttons with Confederate symbols, they were tried as traitors, books were destroyed, and every manner of humiliation known to humanity was inflected upon Asheville citizens.[xciii]

The *Confederate Veteran*, gives some additional information on the Asheville surrender: "Asheville,NC was probably the only town in the Confederacy that the Federals wanted badly and did not capture. It baffled and held in check its besiegers until the very last… it was then ignobly taken possession of in violation of a truce after the soldiery had dispersed and gone to their homes." [xciv]

The enigma of the Asheville skirmish, engagement, surrender, or whatever term one selects to use, is simple: gross misunderstanding. Many of the people committing these base acts were **not Union military personnel.** A large number of these men were deserters, sentinels, "burners," and other assorted non military personnel.[xcv] Many citizens of Asheville blamed the Third Mounted Infantry, Colonel Kirk, and other legitimate Union military for the problems herein described. They may have been in the area, but they were **not** harassing local citizens in the manner above described. Colonel George W. Kirk officially resigned his commission on May 15, 1865, and mustered out of the United States Army on August 8, 1865.[xcvi] This would seem to somewhat negate many of the charges against Colonel Kirk and the Third Mounted Infantry.

As stated earlier, Colonel Kirk and the Third Mounted Infantry were sent to Rabun Gap by way of Waynesville and Franklin, on orders from General Tillson. General Stoneman wanted things "wrapped up" so to speak. Asheville was now under federal control. Colonel Kirk, along with the Second Mounted Infantry, under the command of Colonel William Bartlett, was sent to scour the area. Near Waynesville, a detachment of Colonel Bartlett's command came into contact with a force led by Colonel J.R. Love. Colonel Bartlett had occupied Waynesville with little resistance. General William Thomas hoped to trap Bartlett in Waynesville. He sent for Colonel Love to assist. To bring Colonel Love into action, Thomas sent Lieutenant Robert T. Conley and his company of sharp shooters. Lieutenant Conley was part of General Jubal Early's Raid on Washington force. Colonel Kirk was out of contact with the Second Mounted Infantry. The result was a total rout of the federal detachment. One soldier in the Second Mounted Infantry was killed, a Private by the name of Arwood. As far as is known, Arwood was the last Civil War soldier killed east of the Mississippi River.

On May 7, Colonel Bartlett was faced with the capture of his entire regiment. A conference was held with General Martin. It was finally agreed that General Martin could not hope to accomplish anything by capturing Colonel Bartlett's regiment. On May 9, General Martin and his forces signed parole documents and slowly returned home.[xcvii]

The dates on these events are debatable. Barrett's *Civil War in North Carolina* states: "dates are as variable as the accounts of the skirmish."[xcviii]

This is, without doubt, a true statement. The Third Mounted Infantry returned to Asheville on May 17, 1865. The capture and occupation of Asheville effectively ended the Civil War in the mountains as far as the North Carolina Third Mounted Infantry Vols.(U.S.) under the command of Colonel George Washington Kirk was concerned.[xcix]

RESOLUTIONS

Could anyone deny that the soldiers of the North Carolina Third Mounted Infantry Volunteers were men of courage, forthrightness, and determination? Any reader, present or future, of this history must admit these men did not lack resolve to act on their convictions. It was not an easy thing to leave their families, friends, and neighbors to join an army that was considered the enemy by most standards in the South. Many of these men would pay a high price for this decision. In some cases, the price would be their life. Most, if not all, of these soldiers would be outcasts, to a degree for the remainder of their lives. The family they left to join the army often times, did not welcome them when they returned home. This is a sad, but undeniable fact.

The famous Civil War reference book, used in this history, William F. Fox, *Regimental Losses,* does **not** include the Third Mounted Infantry death statistical figures. Ironically, it includes the Confederate Army, in some cases, and also all of the Union forces. Were these men not consequential enough to be noted even in death? **All** of these soldiers were volunteers. There were no draftees or conscripts in this regiment. In truth, if one conducts any research on the Civil War, he will soon discover that to many historians, the Western Carolinas, and Southwestern Virginia had no Civil War events worth mentioning apart from Stoneman's Raid, and occasional run-ins with Confederate General Breckinridge. One would think the entire war was conducted in Northern Virginia and a few other infrequently mentioned parts of the nation, but certainly not the Western Carolinas. If we ignore the fighting around Knoxville, Eastern Tennessee, as well, would hardly be mentioned.

The men in the Third Mounted Infantry, and all other regiments of volunteers fighting in the Union Army from the western Carolinas, Tennessee, and Southwestern Virginia, exhibited a brand of independence lost in this nation. Not since the Revolutionary War has such independence been noted. These soldiers were patriots and were not going to be told "what to do" by some authority in Richmond, Atlanta, or some other distant city. Just as the "Over mountain Men" came to fight in the Battle of Kings Mountain in 1780, the Third Mounted Infantry came to fight in Asheville, Russellville, Waynesville, etc. These men were not going to be dictated to by anyone. It has been said," nothing is harder than the softness of indifference." These men were certainly not indifferent to their situation.

24

They were not going to cooperate with the inevitable. They joined the Federal Army in an attempt to regain their rightful place in the United States. It worked.

A fact that should denote universal gloom, is the certainty that many citizens of the Western Carolinas, Eastern Tennessee, and Southwestern Virginia are unaware that their states had any participation in the Union army. An example of this fact is that if one mentions the Third Mounted Infantry of North Carolina, the reply is, "didn't they surrender at Appomattox?" One may even receive this reply from historians. Another example is the fact that the North Carolina Department of Archives, while extremely complete, and very efficient to all details, has no records of the Union volunteers from North Carolina.

The above mentioned lack of acknowledgment is understandable given the status these soldiers have received in the past 135 years. It is to be hoped that this situation is about to change. A North Carolina historian of great rank, Dr. Richard Current, has written a book that is used in this history, *Lincoln's Loyalists.* Dr. Current's book is attentive to all the Southern states and the men who volunteered for the Union army. In time perhaps these men will receive the honor and recognition they so richly deserve.

THIRD MOUNTED INFANTRY REGIMENT
OF NORTH CAROLINA VOLUNTEERS (US)
REGIMENTAL STAFF c

1. Colonel George W. Kirk

2. Lieutenant Colonel Robert W. Hubbard

3. Major William W. Rollins

4. Captain John W. Edwards
5. Captain Laban W. McInturff
6. Captain William W. Moore
7. Captain Robert J. Morrison
8. Captain John H. Ray
9. Captain Stephen Street
10. Captain William B. Underwood

11. First Lieutenant George H. Brown
12. First Lieutenant James Hartley
13. First Lieutenant William A. Patterson
14. First Lieutenant William G. Rand
15. First Lieutenant Charles T. Sutphen
16. First Lieutenant Aaron Vancanon

17. Second Lieutenant David C. Cook
18. Second Lieutenant Robert J. Cummings
19. Second Lieutenant William W. Hubbard
20. Second Lieutenant William A. Rucker
21. Second Lieutenant Michael J. Rucker
22. Second Lieutenant James G. Wilson

23. Dr. Marion Roberts, Surgeon
24. Dr. Samuel S.M. Doak, Assistant Surgeon

i *Official Army Register of Volunteer Forces of the United States Army, For the Years 1861-1865,* Part IV (West Virginia, Virginia, North Carolina,

South Carolina, Georgia, Alabama, Mississippi, Louisiana, Texas, Arkansas, Tennessee, Kentucky), Adjutant General's Office, 1865, p. 1148.

BIOGRAPHY OF GEORGE WASHINGTON KIRK

George Washington Kirk was born in Greene County, Tennessee on June 25, 1837. Kirk was born in what is commonly referred to as the Southside of the county, near the North Carolina-Tennessee state line. His father was Alexander Kirk, born about 1814. Alexander Kirk lists his occupation as a bootmaker. His net worth is listed as $250. This is a significant sum, given the time and place.[ci] Sarah Jane Kirk was the mother of George Kirk. Mrs. Kirk died in 1858.This probably was more difficult than normal for George, due to the fact that he was the oldest of eight children and not yet married. One would assume that he probably felt compelled to assist with the upbringing of his brothers and sisters.[cii]

George received a liberal education for the period of history in which he was maturing to manhood. He was a student at least until age 13. This was probably not the norm given the period of history in which George was a youth.[ciii] There is no evidence that George Kirk attended college or received formal education beyond public school. George's occupation before the war is listed as a carpenter. There seems to be little elaboration on this facet of his life.[civ]

On February 28, 1860, George married Maria L. Jones of Greeneville, Tennessee. The Kirks were married at Richland Creek, near Greeneville, by a Reverend Brantley, an Episcopal minister. Maria was born about 1839. George and Maria remained married the rest of their lives.[cv] George and Maria's first child, John, was born May 10, 1861. This preceded the military service career of George Kirk.[cvi]

George Kirk enlisted in the military on August 1, 1862. He joined the First Tennessee Regiment of Volunteers as a private. At some point around the beginning of the year 1863, George was discharged from the First Tennessee to accept a promotion as a Lieutenant in the Fourth Tennessee. Kirk served in that position until June 30, 1863. He was again discharged to accept a promotion as a Captain of Company A, Fifth East Tennessee Cavalry Volunteers. On February 29, 1864, Captain Kirk was transferred to the North Carolina Second Mounted Infantry, and promoted to Major. On June 11, 1864, Kirk was transferred to the newly formed Third Mounted Infantry. At some point, after June 1864, Kirk was promoted to Lieutenant Colonel. On March 14, 1865, George Kirk was promoted to Colonel of the Third Mounted Infantry of North Carolina Volunteers.[cvii] Colonel Kirk was mustered out the of military on August 8, 1865.[cviii]

Colonel Kirk's second and final son, William T.S. Kirk, was born March 28, 1865,[cix] as the war was coming to an end. Like most veterans, Colonel Kirk had to decide what he would do with the rest of his life. For a brief period of time, Kirk settled in Asheville, North Carolina. He later opened a store in Rutherfordton, North Carolina. He soon, however, returned to Washington County, Tennessee and became a farmer. In 1867, he received a commission in the Tennessee militia and commanded a regiment that occupied both Jackson and Overton counties.[cx] The occupation was carried out in an attempt to control KKK activities.

Many people in North Carolina, primarily those in sympathy with the Republican party, felt that the Governor, William Holden, was lax in his dealings with the KKK, and that the Klan was operating in direct violation of the Reconstruction Acts passed by the Republican Congress in Washington. In an attempt to correct this situation, Governor Holden declared martial law and suspended the *Writ of Habeas Corpus*. It was felt that this would end, or at the least, control Klan activities in North Carolina.[cxi]

George Kirk was commissioned to raise a regiment of North Carolina militia by Governor Holden. In an attempt to control Klan activities, Alamance and Caswell counties were virtually taken over by the Kirk regiment. Governor Holden was impeached. Kirk was now the target of legal retaliation. Hoping to avoid his arrest by the national government, federal charges were dismissed against Kirk. He turned himself over to federal authorities, and fled North Carolina to avoid state charges. This situation became a quagmire of legal and political problems for George Kirk.[cxii]

In the fall of 1870, Kirk left the mountain area and moved to Washington, DC. He worked in security for historic buildings and monuments, later as a member of the Washington, DC police department. Kirk was able to secure a position with the United States Patent Office.[cxiii] Kirk remained in the Washington area until at least the year 1881.

George Kirk returned to mountain area of North Carolina and Tennessee. He engaged in the mining industry. It has been said that he made, and lost considerable sums of money during this period of his life. No reliable source could be located to confirm or dispute this accusation.

About 1898, Colonel Kirk began to experience health problems. He had what may have been a heart attack, or perhaps angina problems. In addition, he developed kidney problems, possibly related to his heart condition. This would have ended an active life for most men in their sixties. However, George Kirk was not most men! Kirk moved to California and continued his mining ventures.[cxiv]

Life had changed in the Appalachian/Smoky Mountains since George Kirk's birth in the 1830s. The Civil War, Reconstruction, and slavery had long ago ended. Now, a host of new and very complex problems existed. To a large degree, George Kirk would never be a factor in the solution to these problems. In retrospect, one cannot but ponder how he must have felt toward the end of his life. Would things have been different if he had joined the Confederate Army? His fame would have been legend, given the way he conducted his military duties. Instead, he became a footnote in the history of the Great War of the American people.

Colonel George Washington Kirk surrendered the battle for this life on February 17, 1905, at Gilroy, California. The Colonel was survived by his spouse and two sons. The Gilroy *Advocate* of February 18, 1905, gives only five lines to the Colonel's death.[cxv] This tragic omission is much like the verse in the Biblical book of Ecclesiastes: "that which hath been is now; and that which is to be hath already been...."

NAME INDEX FOR EACH COMPANY

The names of soldiers in each Company are given in alphabetical order. The Companies are also listed in alphabetical order: A-K. The Company Captain (or Lieutenant) is listed first, followed by the Company staff. These men are listed by rank and service. The private soldiers follow in alphabetical order.

There are omissions in this listing. Even though the National Archives supplied the best available copies of the Regiment, some of the names are illegible. This is due to folds in the originals, ink stains, stains of unknown nature, poor handwriting of the Company clerk, to mention but a few of the causes. Also, to decipher some of the writing required immense amounts of time and effort. Apologies are hereby given for incorrect spelling, misprints, and any other errors in listing the names of the soldiers. It was totally accidental.

A separation page with the Company letter designation is included to delineate each Company. Desertions, deaths, transfers, etc., are noted if the information was listed by the Company clerk.

COMPANY A
67 VOLUNTEERS

Staff

1. Captain John W. Edwards, age 27, enlisted September 1864, at Knoxville, TN.
2. Sergeant William Bradshaw, age 37, enlisted June 1864, at Knoxville, TN.
3. Sergeant Benjamin S. Whitten, age 25, enlisted October 1864, at Bulls Gap, TN.
4. Sergeant Thomas M. Rankin, age 23, enlisted July 1864, at Knoxville, TN.
5. Sergeant Abraham McFalls, age 29, enlisted June 1864, at Elizabethton, TN.
6. Sergeant Henry Aeswes, age 29, enlisted June 1864, at Knoxville, TN.
7. Corporal William McSalliand, age 31, enlisted July 1864, at Knoxville, TN.
8. Corporal Samuel Berry, age 23, enlisted August 1864, at Newport, TN.
9. Corporal Joseph Ramsey, age 21,enlisted June 1864, at Knoxville, TN.
10. Corporal Abraham Hensley, age 28, enlisted October 1864, at Bulls Gap, TN.
11. Corporal Frederick Mikles, age 26, enlisted June 1864, at Knoxville, TN.
12. Corporal William Carnes, age 18, enlisted June 1864, at Knoxville, TN.
13. Corporal James Guinn, age 24, enlisted March 1864, at Jonesboro, TN.
14. Corporal Thomas Bryant, age 38, enlisted April 1864, at Burnsville, NC.
15. Musician Henry Bonner, age 16, enlisted August 1864, at Jonesboro, TN.
16. Teamster Satoir Divinia, age 27, enlisted June 1864, at Knoxville, TN

PRIVATE SOLDIERS

1. Andrew Allen, age 18, enlisted August 1864, at Jonesboro, TN.
2. George Allen, age 19, enlisted August 1864, at Jonesboro, TN.
3. Irwin Alien, age 17, enlisted August 1864, at Jonesboro, TN.
4. Thomas Boone, age 22, enlisted June 1864, at Knoxville, TN.
5. Jacob L. Brown, additional information is not available.
6. James M. Brown, age 21, enlisted April 1864, at Jonesboro, TN.
7. Jeremiah Bryan, age 17, enlisted April 1864, at Knoxville, TN.
8. Stephen Cannon, age 24, enlisted June 1864, at Knoxville, TN.

9. Harrison Church, age 28, enlisted June 1864, at Knoxville, TN.
10. John Clanton, age 30, enlisted November 1864, at Knoxville, TN.
11. Solomon Collins, age 24, enlisted June 1864, at Knoxville, TN.
12. Francis Ervine, age 18, enlisted July 1864, at Knoxville, TN.
13. John M. Fowler, age 18, enlisted June 1864, at Knoxville, TN.
14. Joseph B. Franklin, age 23, enlisted June 1864, at Knoxville, TN.
15. William Y. Good, age 17, enlisted August 1864, at Jonesboro, TN.
16. Columbus Graham, age 18, enlisted November 1864, at Knoxville, TN.
17. James C. Hewitt, age 33, enlisted September 1864, at Bulls Gap, TN.
18. Isaac Hice, age 17, enlisted May 1864, at Knoxville, TN.
19. John Hice, age 18, enlisted May 1864, at Knoxville, TN.
20. William R. Hickman, age 17, enlisted July 1864, at Elizabethton, TN.
21. John Higgins, age 22, enlisted June 1864, at Knoxville, TN.
22. Joel A. Hollifield, age 20, enlisted June 1864, at Knoxville, TN.
23. William M. Hollifield, age 18, enlisted June 1864, at Knoxville, TN.
24. Jesse Howell, age 20, enlisted October 1864, at Bulls Gap, TN.
25. Swinfield Howell, age 22, enlisted October 1824, at Bulls Gap, TN.
26. Jubal Huskins, age 41, enlisted March 1864, at Jonesboro, TN.
27. William C. Huskins, age 29, enlisted March 1864, at Jonesboro, TN.
28. Edward Jackson, age 18, enlisted October 1864, at Bulls Gap, TN.
29. Levi Jonis, age 37, enlisted June 1864, at Knoxville, TN.
30. David S. Laws, age 33, enlisted June 1864, at, Knoxville, TN.
31. James S. Laws, age 18, enlisted June 1864, at Jonesboro, TN.
32. David S. Lewis, age 33, enlisted June 1864, at Knoxville, TN.
33. Henry Matthews, age 44, enlisted June 1864, at Knoxville, TN.
34. John Matthews, age 43, enlisted June 1864, at Knoxville, TN.
35. William B. McMahan, age 34, enlisted July 1864, at Burnsville, NC.
36. Archibald Micheal, age 24, enlisted October 1864, at Knoxville, TN.
37. Columbus Miller, age 27, enlisted June 1864, at Knoxville, TN.
38. John Miller, age 39, enlisted March 1864, at Jonesboro, TN.
39. James Ray, age 18, enlisted October 1864, at Knoxville, TN.
40. Lewis A. Roninger, age 18, enlisted June 1864, at Knoxville, TN.
41. Isaac Salor, age 18, enlisted July 1864, at Strawberry Plains, TN.
42. Samuel Sander, age 19, enlisted July 1864, at Elizabethton, TN.
43. James E. Shehan, age 21, enlisted June 1864, at Knoxville, TN.
44. Leander Simmons, age 44, enlisted June 1864, at Knoxville, TN.
45. Samuel Sittle, age 18, enlisted August 1864, at Jonesboro, TN.
46. John E. Smith, age 18, enlisted June 1864, at Knoxville, TN.
47. Lewis M. Sparks, age 18, enlisted October 1864, at Bulls Gap, TN.

48. Jacob Tapp, age 19, enlisted December 1864, at Knoxville, TN.
49. Vincent Tapp, age 25, enlisted December 1864, at Knoxville, TN.
50. Charles Tipton, age 18, enlisted June 1864, at Knoxville, TN.
51. Jacob Tipton, age 19, enlisted May 1864, at Jonesboro, TN.

Co b

STAFF

1. Captain Laban W. McIntuoff, age_, enlisted August 1864, at Knoxville, TN.
2. Sergeant Joseph M. Britain, age 25, enlisted 1864, at Strawberry Plains, TN.
3. Sergeant Andrew J. Brown, age 35, enlisted June 1864, at Knoxville, TN.
4. Sergeant Thomas L. Bovin, age 19, enlisted July 1864, at Knoxville, TN.
5. Sergeant David A. Harmon, age 33, enlisted July 1864, at Knoxville, TN.
6. Sergeant James Revise, age 23, enlisted July 1864, at Knoxville, TN.
7. Corporal John K. Good, age 17, enlisted July 1864, at Knoxville, TN.
8. Corporal John. Hockney, age 27, enlisted July 1864, at Knoxville, TN.
9. Corporal John Rouse, age 25, enlisted July 1864, at Knoxville, TN.
10. Corporal John O. Howell, age 23, enlisted October 1864, at Bulls Gap, TN.
11. Corporal Wiley M. Hanson, age 27, enlisted July 1864, at Knoxville, TN.
12. Corporal Jacob Brown, age 24, enlisted June 1864, at Knoxville, TN.
13. Corporal Sidney G. Hollon, age 31, enlisted July 1864, at Knoxville, TN.
14. Corporal Daniel Haun, age 20, enlisted August 1864, at Knoxville, TN.
15. Musician Samuel Hayney, age 22, enlisted June 1864, at Strawberry Plains, TN.
16. Musician James M. Shands, age 31, enlisted July 1864, at Knoxville, TN.
17. Teamster Alfred Wilson, age 35, enlisted July 1864, at Knoxville.

PRIVATE SOLDIERS

1. John S. Anderson was charged with desertion. The charge was later removed. Private Anderson was ordered to apply for discharge. No other information was given.
2. John Barnett was charged with desertion, the charge was removed. Private Barnett was ordered to apply for discharge. Private Barnett was a company cook.
3. John Bennett, age 22, enlisted in June 1864, at Knoxville, TN. Private Bennett was the Company cook.

4. William R. Bivins, age 22, enlisted July 1864, at Strawberry Plains, TN. Private Bivins died of fever July 19, 1865, in a Knoxville hospital.
5. William Billings, age 36, enlisted July 1864.
6. William P. Blackwell, age 21, enlisted June 1864, at Strawberry Plains, TN.
7. ___ Blackwell, age 18, enlisted July 1864, at Knoxville, TN.
8. ___ Brockshin, age 24, enlisted October 1864, at Bulls Gap, TN.
9. John Eller, age 25, enlisted July 1864, at Knoxville, TN. Private Eller died in a Knoxville hospital in 1866 of a war related illness.
10. Thomas Eller, age 18, enlisted July 1864, at Knoxville, TN. Private Eller was taken prisoner by the Confederate Army November 15, 1864.
11. ___ Gay, age 19, enlisted August 1864, at Knoxville, TN.
12. Miles Gofourth, age 19, enlisted August 1864, at Knoxville, TN.
13. ___ Gosnell, age 34, enlisted June 1864, at Strawberry Plains, TN.
14. Johnny B. Gosnell, age 23, enlisted June 1864, at Strawberry Plains, TN.
15. Solomon Gray, age 18, enlisted February 1865, at Yadkinville, NC.
16. Jesse Hall, age 19, enlisted June 1864, at Strawberry Plains, TN.
17. John L. Hampton, age 16, enlisted June 1864, at Strawberry Plains, TN.
18. Lundy Hampton, age 44, enlisted June 1864, at Strawberry Plains, TN.
19. Lawson R. Harmon, age 31, enlisted July 1864, at Strawberry Plains, TN.
20. Emanuel Harris, age 44, enlisted July 1864, at Strawberry Plains, TN.
21. Peter Haun, age 18, enlisted March 1864, at Knoxville, TN.
22. English Hayworth, age 43, enlisted June 1864, at Strawberry Plains, TN.
23. William Hayworth, age 24, enlisted June 1864, at Strawberry Plains, TN.
24. Solomon Heaney, age 22, enlisted October 1864, at Strawberry Plains, TN.
25. Ancg C. Howell, age 25, enlisted October 1864, at Strawberry Plains, TN.
26. George W. Howett, age 18, enlisted February 1865, at Wilksboro, NC.
27. William Johnson, age 18, enlisted February 1865, at _____.
28. Williamson Johnson, age 42, enlisted July 1864, at Knoxville, TN.
29. Ambrose Lawing, age 40, enlisted July 1864, at Strawberry Plains, TN.
30. Elbert Lawing, age 19, enlisted July 1864, at Strawberry Plains, TN.
31. Thomas Loyd, age 24, enlisted August 1864, at Strawberry Plains, TN.
32. John McIntosh, age 26, enlisted July 1864, at Knoxville, TN.
33. Berry Mitchell, age 40, enlisted June 1864, at Knoxville, TN. Private Mitchell was the company cook.

34. Money Howell, (no information given) Private Howell died June 16, 1865 from brain inflammation in a Knoxville, TN hospital.
35. Anderson Moore, age 18, enlisted August 1864, at Knoxville, TN.
36. Thomas E. Moore, age 27, enlisted June 1864, at Strawberry Plains, TN.
37. Alvin Newton, age 22, enlisted June 1864, at Knoxville, TN.
38. Morris Newton, age 17, (no other information given). Private Newton was charged with desertion. The charge was later removed. Private Newton was killed in action on October 28, 1864.
39. Joseph L. Padget, age 30, enlisted July 1864, at Knoxville, TN. Private Padget was discharged May 19, 1865, for medical reasons.
40. Jackson Peck, age 25, enlisted June 1864, at Knoxville, TN.
41. George W. Perkins, age 18, enlisted June 1864, at Strawberry Plains, TN.
42. George W. Price, age 19, enlisted June 1864, at Strawberry Plains, TN.
43. Alfred W. Rank, age 21, enlisted June 1864, at Knoxville, TN. Private Rank died in the service of his country. No cause is given.
44. Daniel Reece, age 18, enlisted June 1864, at Strawberry Plains, TN.
45. Henry C. Reece, age 42, enlisted June 1864, at Strawberry Plains, TN.
46. John P. Reese, age 19, enlisted October 1864, at Knoxville, TN.
47. Albert G. Rowe, age 21, enlisted March 1864, at Knoxville, TN. Charged with desertion. The charge was later removed. No other information is given.
48. Robert B. Sams, age 30, enlisted July 1864, at Knoxville, TN.
49. Rebon Sparks, age 21, enlisted August 1864, at Knoxville, TN. Charged with desertion September 20, 1864, at Bulls Gap, TN.
50. Calvin Shinalle, age 22, enlisted June 1864, at Knoxville, TN.
51. Christian Shore, age 23, enlisted August 1864, at Knoxville, TN.
52. Samuel Shore, age 21, enlisted August 1864, at Knoxville, TN.
53. Mark H. Shremake, age 25, enlisted September 1864, at Bulls Gap, TN.
54. Samuel Simmons, age 20, enlisted October 1864, at Greeneville, TN.
55. Edwin Sinks, age 20, enlisted August 1864, at Knoxville, TN.
56. Elkana L. Slackleather, age 18, enlisted July 1864, at Knoxville, TN.
57. John Slackleather, age 19, enlisted July 1864, at Knoxville, TN.
58. Gideon Smart. No other legible information is given.
59. Francis Smith, age 23, enlisted January 1865, at Watauga, NC.
60. Hanbiks Studivants, age 19, enlisted July 1864, at Knoxville, TN.
61. John Swangan, age 19, enlisted August 1864, at Knoxville, TN. Private Swangan was charged with desertion on September 20, 1864, at Bulls Gap TN.

62. Albert Tipton, age 20, enlisted June 1864, at Knoxville, TN. Private Tipton was charged with desertion on June 23, 1865, at Greeneville, TN.
63. Steven Tompkins, age 32, enlisted June 1864, at Knoxville, TN.

64. Darby Triplet, age 19, enlisted August 1864, at Knoxville, TN.
65. Moses Triplet, age 18, enlisted August 1864, at Knoxville, TN.
66. Moses D. Tucker, age 34, enlisted August 1864, at Knoxville, TN.
67. David Weasiner, age 19, enlisted July 1864, at Knoxville, TN.
68. James Wells, age 35, enlisted June 1864, at Knoxville, TN. Private well was one of the company cooks.
69. Leanier A. White, age 35, enlisted July 1864, at Knoxville, TN.
70. William White, age 38, enlisted March 1864, at Knoxville, TN.
71. John William, age 18, enlisted July 1864, at Knoxville, TN.
72. William B. Wilson, age 26, enlisted June 1824, at Knoxville, TN. Private Wilson was charged with desertion September 23, 1865, at Greeneville, TN.
73. Riley W. Worden, age 20, enlisted August 1864, at Knoxville, TN. Private Worden was charged with desertion August 4, 1864, at Strawberry Plains, TN.

Co c

STAFF

1. Lieutenant William Patterson, age 33, enlisted March 1865, at Knoxville, TN.
2. Robert Morrison, First Lieutenant, age _____, enlisted September 1864, at Knoxville, TN. Lieutenant Morrison was Transferred from the company. No date was given.
3. Second Lieutenant Michael J. Sprinkle, age 31, enlisted December 1864, at Knoxville, TN.
4. First Sergeant Albert W. Fullam, age 29, enlisted September 1864, at Bulls Gap, TN.
5. Sergeant Thomas M. Parker, age 27, enlisted May 1864, at Knoxville, TN.
6. Sergeant James H. Wheeler, age 35, enlisted September 1864, at Knoxville, TN.
7. Sergeant John D. Goolsby, age 22, enlisted August 1864, at Morristown, TN.
8. Sergeant Hughey Gedswood, age 26, enlisted April 1864, at Paint Rock, NC.
9. Corporal John H. Ballard, age 20, enlisted September 1864, at Bulls Gap, TN.
10. Corporal Samuel Ealeris, age 23, enlisted June 1864, at Knoxville, TN.
11. Corporal Joshua Heran, age 18, enlisted September 1864, at Bulls Gap, TN.
12. Corporal James M. Watts, age 23, enlisted June 1864, at Morristown, TN.
13. Corporal Daniel T. Harbin, age 18, enlisted October 1864, at Bulls Gap, TN.
14. Corporal James M. Erwin, age 18, enlisted August 1864, at Strawberry Plains, TN.
15. Corporal Samuel B. Erwin, age 18, enlisted August 1864, at Strawberry Plains, TN.

PRIVATE SOLDIERS

1. Henry H. Becis, age 19, enlisted September 1864, at Bulls Gap, TN.
2. John S. Beck, age 18, enlisted September 1864, at Bulls Gap, TN.
3. Columbus Blackburn, age 27, enlisted March 1865, at Knoxville, TN.

4. Noah Blankenship, age_____, enlisted 1865, at Knoxville, TN. Private Blankenship was charged with desertion. No information was given as to the circumstances.
5. Riley W. Bowen, age 18, enlisted October 1864, at Bulls Gap, TN.
6. George Brooks, age 26, enlisted September 1864, at Bulls Gap, TN.
7. James Brooks, age 18, enlisted September 1864, at Bulls Gap, TN.
8. Noah Buckner, age 22, enlisted March 1865, at Knoxville, TN.
9. William Capps, age 22, enlisted October 1864, at Bulls Gap, TN. Capps was promoted to corporal. Corporal Capps died in the service of his country. No date is given.
10. Silas G. Clark, age 26, enlisted June 1864, at Knoxville, TN.
11. Jefferson D. Coatts, age 22, enlisted June 1864, at Knoxville, TN.
12. James H. Cordell, age 21, enlisted June 1864, at Knoxville, TN. Private Cordell was discharged in June of 1865 for medical reasons.
13. Jackson Davis, age ___, enlisted March 1864, at Bulls Gap, TN. Private Davis was charged with desertion. Circumstances are not given.
14. William M. Dover, age 24, enlisted October 1864, at Bulls Gap, TN.
15. Ephraim Elder, age 19, enlisted August 1864, at Bulls Gap, TN. Private Elder died in the service of his country. No date is given.
16. John Erwin, age 18, enlisted August 1864, at Strawberry Plains, TN.
17. Henry Franks, age 30, enlisted July 1864, at Knoxville, TN. Private Franks was captured by the Confederate Army in Cocke County, TN. in 1864. No other information is given.
18. William Fisher, age 19, enlisted 1864, at Knoxville, TN.
19. Hiram Gentry, age 19, enlisted September 1864, at Bulls Gap, TN. Private Gentry died in the service of his country. No is date given.
20. Albert E. Girlie, age _____, enlisted 1864, at Bulls Gap, TN. Private Girlie was charged with desertion. Circumstances are not given.
21. Benjamin Grant, age _____, enlisted 1864, at Bulls Gap, TN. Private Grant was charged with desertion. Circumstances are not given.
22. Samuel W. Hard, age 22, enlisted July 1864, at Knoxville, TN.
23. Benjamin Henderson, age 20, enlisted September 1864, at Knoxville, TN.
24. William C. Henderson, 18, enlisted September 1864, at Bulls Gap, TN.
25. Andrew Hensley, age _____, enlisted July 1864, at Knoxville, TN.
26. Clingman Hensley, age 18, enlisted November 1864, at Knoxville, TN.
27. Lorezo Hensley, age 19, enlisted November 1864, at Knoxville, TN.
28. Riley A. Hill, age ____, enlisted September 1864, at Knoxville, TN. Private Hill was charged with desertion. No circumstances are given.

29. Isaac Holcombe, age 18, enlisted March 1865, at Knoxville, TN.

30. William Hughey, age 18, enlisted October 1864, at Bulls Gap, TN.

31. O. Jackson, age_____, enlisted___, at _____. Private Jackson was charged with desertion. No circumstances are given.

32. Eli H. Jarett, age 25, enlisted June 1864, at Knoxville, TN.

33. Chinkin Kennemeur, age_____, enlisted 1864, at Bulls Gap, TN. Private Kennemeur was charged with desertion. No circumstances are given.

34. John Kennemeur, age 18, enlisted September 1864, at Bulls Gap, TN.

35. Marlin A. King, age 22, enlisted December 1864, at Knoxville, TN.

36. Joseph Ledford, age____, enlisted September 1864, at Bulls Gap, TN. Private Ledford was charged with desertion at Bulls Gap, Tn. No date or circumstances are given.

37. Samuel McLure, age 28, enlisted September 1864, at Bulls Gap, TN.

38. Robert McMahan, age 18, enlisted August 1864, at _____. Private McMahan died in the service of his country. No date or circumstance is given.

39. David Nabb, age 44, enlisted October 1864, at _____. Private Nabb was charged with desertion at Knoxville, TN. No date or circumstance is given.

40. John F. Noriss, age 22, enlisted December 1864, at Knoxville, TN.

41. John Odell, age 44, enlisted August 1864, at Morristown, TN.

42. R.J. Oliver. No information is given on Private Oliver. Private Oliver was charged with desertion. No date or circumstance is given.

43. Adolphus Pain, age 21, enlisted September 1864, at Knoxville, TN.

44. John T. Parker, age 42, enlisted May 1864, at Knoxville, TN.

45. Robert Penland, age 35, enlisted March 1864, at Knoxville, TN.

46. James Perry, age 38, enlisted September 1864, at Knoxville, TN.

47. Robert J. Ponder, age 35, enlisted March 1865, at Knoxville, TN.

48. Alfred Rector, age 19, enlisted August 1864, at Morristown, TN.

49. Elehright Rector, age 41, enlisted August 1864, at Morristown, TN.

50. Franklin Rector, age 30, enlisted September 1864, at Greeneville, TN.

51. Julias Rector, age 18, enlisted August 1864, at Morristown, TN.

52. William Rector, age 18, enlisted March 1865, at Knoxville, TN.

53. David Redmond, age 18, enlisted March 1865, at Knoxville, TN.

54. George Ramsey Reslored, no additional information is given. Private Reslored is charged with desertion. No date or circumstance is given.

55. James Ramsey Reslored, no additional information is given. Private Reslored is charged with desertion. No date or circumstance is given.

56. Shaderic Reslored, no additional information is given. Private Reslored is charged with desertion. No date or circumstance is given.
57. Edmond Rice, age 19, enlisted June 1864, at Knoxville, TN.
58. Isace Rice, age 18, enlisted August 1864, at Morristown, TN. Private Rice died in the service of his country. No date or circumstance is given.
59. Henry Roberts, age 19, enlisted June 1864, at Knoxville, TN.
60. Martin Roberts, age 22, enlisted March 1864, at Bulls Gap TN. Private Roberts was captured by the Confederate Army. No date or circumstance is given.
61. William Roberts, age 38, enlisted June 1864, at Knoxville, TN. Private Roberts died in the service of his country. No date or circumstance is given.
62. James Robertson, age 18, enlisted March 1864, at Bulls Gap, TN.
63. Ephriam Smith, age 44, enlisted January 1865, at Knoxville, TN.
64. John Smith, age 18, enlisted January 1865, at Knoxville, TN.
65. Joseph Smith, age 18, enlisted October 1864, at Bulls Gap, TN.
66. William Sopsher, age 18, enlisted November 1864, at Knoxville, TN.
67. Edwin Teague, age 24, enlisted March 1865, at Knoxville, TN.
68. William Watts, no information is given. Private Watts is charged with desertion. No date or circumstance is given.
69. Seander West, age 15, enlisted September 1864, at Knoxville, TN.
70. William James West, age 19, enlisted March 1864, at Bulls Gap, TN.
71. William P. West, age 19, enlisted November 1864, at Knoxville, TN.
72. James Wheeler, age 18, enlisted July 1864, at Knoxville, TN. Private Wheeler died in the service of his country. No date or circumstance is given.
73. Jacob Wild, age 20, enlisted June 1864, at Knoxville, TN.
74. John M. Wild, age 23, enlisted June 1864, at Knoxville, TN.
75. Mitchell Willson, age 25, enlisted March 1865, at Knoxville, TN.
76. Henry Worley, age 27, enlisted September 1864, at Knoxville, TN.
77. Joseph Worley, age 21, enlisted September 1864, Knoxville, TN.
78. William Wright, age 18, enlisted October 1864, at Knoxville, TN. Private Wright is charged with desertion. No date or circumstance is given.

Co d

STAFF

1. Captain William H. Kirk, no other information is given.
2. First Sergeant Ezekill Hensley, age 25, enlisted August 1864, at Bulls Gap, TN.
3. Sergeant Alfred A. Wyatt, age 20, enlisted August 1864, at Bulls Gap, TN.
4. Sergeant Jesse Worton, age 34, enlisted September 1864, at Yadkinville, NC.
5. Sergeant William B. Widener, age 19, enlisted September, 1864, at Bulls Gap, TN.
6. Sergeant James D. Smith, age 29, enlisted September 1864, at Bulls Gap, TN.
7. First Corporal Isaac Brown, age 44, enlisted June 1864, at Knoxville, TN.
8. Corporal Sovguitta Squirrel, age 20, enlisted June 1864, at Knoxville, TN.
9. Corporal William C. Bovender, age 18, enlisted August 1864, at Knoxville, TN.
10. Corporal Eli Wooten, age 20, enlisted September 1864, at Yadkinville,NC.
11. Corporal David Osturn, age 25, enlisted June 1864, at Jefferson, NC
12. Corporal Enoch B. Prim, age 38, enlisted August 1864, at Knoxville, TN
13. Musician Alfred Ovenby, age 44, enlisted September 1864, at Bulls Gap, TN.
14. Teamster John W. Carter, age 20, enlisted August 1864, at Bulls Gap, TN.

PRIVATE SOLDIERS

1. James A. Aldridge, age 35, enlisted August 1864, at Bulls Gap, TN.
2. James Amistas, age 44, enlisted November 1864, at Knoxville, TN.
3. John Anklook, age 44, enlisted July 1864, at Knoxville, TN.
4. Jasper Bailey, age 22, enlisted August 1864, at Bulls Gap, TN. Private Bailey is charged with desertion. No date or circumstance is given.
5. Williton Baulon, age 27, enlisted March 1864, at Bulls Gap, TN.
6. Benjamin Brown, age 45, enlisted June 1864, at Knoxville, TN.

7. James Burnett, age 18, enlisted November 1864, at Knoxville, TN. Private Burnett is charged with desertion. No date or circumstance is given.
8. James H, Cagle, age 26, enlisted October 1864, at Bulls Gap, TN.
9. Ruben Conner, age 23, enlisted June 1864, at Knoxville, TN. Private Conner is charged with desertion. No date or circumstance is given.
10. William M. Conner, age 21, enlisted September 1864, at Bulls Gap, TN. Private Conner was captured by the Confederate Army, November 13, 1864.
11. James A. Dalton, age 18, enlisted September 1864, at Bulls Gap, TN,
12. Ki Der-las, age 41, enlisted January 1864, at Knoxville, TN.
13. John Di-a, age 34, enlisted June 1864, at Knoxville, TN. Private Di-a died in the service of his country. No date or circumstance is given.
14. E-li Chris, age 22, enlisted June 1864, at Knoxville, TN. Private Chris was promoted to Corporal. The date is not given. Corporal Chris died in the service of his country. No date or circumstance is given.
15. Nathaniel Edwards, age 32, enlisted August 1864, at Wilksboro, NC.
16. Ashberry L. Galloway, age 19, enlisted September 1864, at Transylvania, NC.
17. John I- Got pa, age 18, enlisted August 1864, at Knoxville, TN.
18. Thomas Gragg, age 18, enlisted November 1864, at Knoxville, TN. Private Gragg is charged with desertion. No date or circumstance is given.
19. Augustin E. Head, age 30, enlisted August 1864, at Knoxville, TN.
20. John Helterbrand, age 20, enlisted August 1864, at Knoxville, TN.
21. Joseph Henry, age 28, enlisted October 1864, at Transylvania, NC.
22. James Hobson, age 32, enlisted July 1864, at Knoxville, TN.
23. John Hobson, age 23, enlisted July 1864, at Calhoun, NC.
24. William C. Hobson, age 19, enlisted July 1864, at Knoxville, TN.
25. Finley P. Johnson, age 20, enlisted August 1864, at Wilksboro, NC.
26. Stephen Johnson, age 21, enlisted June 1864, at Knoxville, TN.
27. John_, age 28, enlisted June 1864, at Knoxville, TN. (Note: this is the only name given for this soldier. There does not appear to be any error on the part of the company clerk.)
28. John Kanoh, age 45, enlisted June 1864, at Knoxville, TN.
29. Tataguga Kanoh, age 21, enlisted November 1864, at Knoxville, TN.
30. Thomas Kanoh, age 19, enlisted June 1864, at Knoxville, TN.
31. Jonas Conrad Killian, age 37, enlisted June 1864, at Knoxville, TN.
32. James Lanter, age 19, enlisted June 1864, at Wytheville, VA.

33. Andrew Lanning, age 18, enlisted March 1864, at Bulls Gap, TN.
34. Phil Ledbetter, age 18, enlisted September 1864, at Bulls Gap, TN. Private Ledbetter was captured by the Confederate Army November 13, 1864.
35. Drewy Lewis, age 37, enlisted August 1864, at Knoxville, TN.
36. John L. Logan, age 41, enlisted June 1864, at Knoxville, TN.
37. Francis M. McClure, age 22, enlisted September 1864, at Bulls Gap, TN.
38. Okivabaga, age 44, enlisted November 1864, at Knoxville, TN.(Note: this is the only name given for this soldier. There does not appear to be an error on the part of the company clerk.)
39. John Oalayiway, age 23, enlisted November 1864, at Knoxville, TN.
40. Thomas Oalayiway, age 18, enlisted November 1864, at Knoxville, TN.
41. Ross Oliver, age 18, enlisted October 1864, at Bulls Gap, TN.
42. Benjamin Oter, age 22, enlisted June 1864, at Knoxville, TN.
43. Thomas Oter, age 18, enlisted November 1864, at Knoxville, TN.
44. David Palle, age 40, enlisted 1864, at Knoxville, TN.
45. Chris Patridge, age 18, enlisted July 1864, at Knoxville, TN.
46. Columbus Patridge, age 40, enlisted July 1864, at Knoxville, TN. Private Patridge died in the service of his country. No date or circumstance is given.
47. Lawson Peterson, age 23, enlisted June 1864, at Knoxville, TN.
48. James Porter, age 34, enlisted August 1864, at Knoxville, TN.
49. William Porter, age 22, enlisted August 1864, at Wilksboro, NC. Private Porter is charged with desertion. No date or circumstance is given.
50. Mason Ratliff, age 45, enlisted June 1864, at Knoxville, TN.
51. Alvin E. Rees, age 34, enlisted June 1864, at Knoxville, TN.
52. Thomas Renfrow, age 23, enlisted July 1864, at Calhoun, NC.
53. Alfred Roberts, age 18, enlisted October 1864, at Transylvania, NC.
54. Robert Rutledge, age 28, enlisted September 1864, at Bulls Gap, TN.
55. Samuel Sells, age 37, enlisted September 1864, at Bulls Gap, TN. Private Sells is charged with desertion. No date or circumstance is given.
56. James Sims, age 20, enlisted August 1864, at Knoxville, TN. Private Sims died in the service of his country. No date or circumstance is given.
57. John Soldier, age 24, enlisted June 1864, at Knoxville, TN. Private Soldier died in the service of his country. No date or circumstance is given.
58. Joseph Sutton, age 18, enlisted November 1864, at Knoxville, TN.

59. Abraham Tilson, age 18, enlisted October 1864, at Mitchell, NC. Private Tilson is charged with desertion. No date or circumstance is given.
60. To-i-so-ha, age 22, enlisted June 1864, at Knoxville, TN. Private To-i-so-ha died in the service of his country. No date or circumstance is given.
61. Robert Townsen, age 18, enlisted November 1864, at Knoxville, TN. Private Townsen died in the service of his country. No date or circumstance is given.
62. Den-vi-na, age 34, enlisted June 1864, at Knoxville, TN.
63. John Wadkins, age 28, enlisted July 1864, at Knoxville, TN. Private Wadkins is charged with desertion. No date or circumstance is given.
64. Wail Le, age 19, enlisted June 1864, at Knoxville, TN.
65. John Walker, age 37, enlisted June 1864, at Knoxville, TN.
66. Washington, age 28, enlisted June 1864, at Knoxville, TN. (Note: this is the only name given for this soldier. There does not appear to be an error on the part of the company clerk.)
67. Isaac Whitson, age 29, enlisted July 1864, at Calhoun, NC. Private Whitson is charged with desertion. No date or circumstance is given.
68. John Widenen, age 18, enlisted September 1864, at Bulls Gap, TN.
69. Palson Widenen, age 44, enlisted September 1864, at Bulls Gap, TN.
70. Johnson Wood, age 35, enlisted August 1864, at Transylvania, NC.
71. William Wood, age _, enlisted _, at _.
72. Walkinstick, age 32, enlisted February 1865, at Knoxville, TN.
73. Walkinstick, age 44, enlisted February 1865, at Knoxville, TN.
74. Wy-an-is, age 24, enlisted June 1864, at Knoxville, TN. Private Wy-an-is died in the service of his country. No date or circumstance is given.

Co e

STAFF

1. Captain Stephen Street, age 37, enlisted March 1865, at Knoxville, TN.
2. First Lieutenant Garland Guthradge, age _, enlisted September 1864, Knoxville, TN. Lieutenant Guthradge resigned from the Regiment.
3. Second Lieutenant David Cook, age 21, enlisted March 1865, at Knoxville, TN.
4. First Sergeant Peter A. Frydell, enlisted October 1864, at Bulls Gap, TN.
5. Sergeant Allen R. Case, age 37, enlisted March 1864, at Mitchell County, NC.
6. Sergeant Aldolphus Garren, age 37, enlisted April 1864, at Transylvania, NC.
7. Sergeant John D. Street, age 35, enlisted March 1864, at Mitchell County, NC.
8. Sergeant John D. Taylor, age 24, enlisted October 1864, at Bulls Gap, TN.
9. Corporal George W. Warrick, age 19, enlisted March 1864, at Mitchell County, NC.
10. Corporal John W. Taylor, age 39, enlisted September 1864, at Yancey County, NC.
11. Corporal Michel Byrd, age 19, enlisted September 1864, at Mitchell County, NC.
12. Corporal Anderson D. Garren, age 39, enlisted October 1864, at Hendersonville, NC.
13. Corporal Guthradge Phillips, age 18, enlisted March 1864, at Mitchell County, NC.
14. Corporal Merit H. Gallaway, age 18, enlisted March 1864, at Hendersonville, NC.
15. Corporal Willis Phillips, age 33, enlisted September 1864, at Yancey County, NC.
16. Corporal Leois E. Melton, age 18, enlisted March 1864, at Mitchell County, NC.
17. Musician Joseph L. Gouge, age 19, enlisted March 1864, at Mitchell County, NC.
18. Musician John Riddle, age 34, enlisted July 1864, at Mitchell County, NC.
19. Teamster Nathan Riddle, age 42, enlisted March 1864, at Mitchell County, NC.

PRIVATE SOLDIERS

1. John Barrett, age 39, enlisted November 1864, at Mitchell County, NC.
2. William Bishop, age 34, enlisted March 1864, at Mitchell County, NC. Private Bishop is charged with desertion as of October 29, 1864.
3. Jackson Bowman, age 18, enlisted March 1864, at Mitchell County, NC.
4. Erwin Bradford, no age given, enlisted November 1864, at Knoxville, TN.
5. John Bradford, age 25, enlisted March 1864, at Bulls Gap, TN.
6. Franklin Britt, age 44, enlisted March 1864, at Carter County, TN.
7. John Brown, age 39, enlisted November 1864, at Knoxville, TN.
8. Bethel A. Bryant, age 25, enlisted March 1864, at Mitchell County, NC.
9. Green Y. Buchanan, age 19, enlisted March 1865, at Mitchell County, NC.
10. William A. Buchanan, age 18, enlisted March 1864, at Mitchell County, NC.
11. George Byrd, age 18, enlisted March 1864, at Mitchell County, NC.
12. Phillip Carpenter, age 42, enlisted October 1864, Knoxville, TN.
13. Josiah Chavis, age 26, enlisted August 1864, at Knoxville, TN.
14. Robert Chavis, age 20, enlisted August 1864, at Knoxville, TN.
15. Jackson Cole, age 44, enlisted October 1864, at Bulls Gap, TN.
16. John Cole, age 22, enlisted November 1864, at Bulls Gap, TN.
17. John P. Crook, age 19, enlisted November 1864, at Knoxville, TN.
18. Hugh B. Conn, age 20, enlisted March 1865, at Knoxville, TN.
19. Albert Couch, age 30, enlisted October 1864, at Bulls Gap, TN. Private Couch is charged with desertion March 1, 1865.
20. John P. Crook, age 19, enlisted November 1864, at Knoxville, TN.
21. Jacob Davis, age 39, enlisted March 1864, at Mitchell County, NC.
22. Josiah Davis, age 35, enlisted March 1864, at Mitchell County, NC.
23. John Edwards, age 31, enlisted September 1864, at Yancey County, NC.
24. Robert Edwards, age 22, enlisted September 1864, at Yancey County, NC.
25. Rictas Forbes, age 24, enlisted March 1864, at Mitchell County, NC.
26. William Forbes, age 18, enlisted March 1864, at Mitchell County, NC.
27. Ezekiel Garland, age 18, enlisted March 1864, at Mitchell County, NC.
28. John Garland, age 22, enlisted March 1864, at Mitchell County, NC.
29. Samuel Garland, age 29, enlisted March 1864, at Mitchell County, NC.

30. Mitchell E. Garren, age 18, enlisted September 1864, at Bulls Gap, TN. Private Garren died in the service of his country December 4, 1864, at Knoxville, TN.
31. Samuel C. George, age 18, enlisted March 1864, at Mitchell County, NC.
32. John Gipson, age 35, enlisted November 1864, at Knoxville, TN. Private Gipson is charged with desertion on December 11, 1864.
33. Samuel Gipson, age 27, enlisted November 1864, at Knoxville, TN.
34. Stephen Gipson, age 25, enlisted November 1864, at Knoxville, TN.
35. William Gipson, age 23, enlisted November 1864, at Knoxville, TN.
36. Samuel P. Green, age 18, enlisted March 1864, at Mitchell County, TN. Private Green died in the service of his country on December 6, 1864, at the General Hospital in Knoxville, TN.
37. Lawrence E. Grindstaff, age 24, enlisted March 1864, at Mitchell County, NC.
38. Anthony Harris, age 20, enlisted October 1864, at Bulls Gap, TN. Private Harris is charged with desertion December 29, 1864.
39. Thomas Henson, age 18, enlisted September 1864, at Mitchell County, NC.
40. William Higgins, age 24, enlisted October 1864, at Yancey County, NC.
41. John Hileman, age 25, enlisted March 1864, at Mitchell County, NC.
42. Daniel H. Husk, age 20, enlisted October 1864, at Bulls Gap, TN. Private Husk is charged with desertion on December 3, 1864.
43. John F. Kykendall, age 18, enlisted March 1864, at Mitchell County, NC. Private Kykendall is charged with desertion December 27, 1864.
44. Eli T. Ledwell, age 18, enlisted August 1864, at Knoxville, TN.
45. Robert Lewis, age, 38, enlisted April 1864, at Yancey County, NC.
46. Warren J. Lockman, age 26, enlisted January 1865, at Brabston Mills, TN.
47. Frederick L. Loftis, age 18, enlisted October 1864, at Knoxville, TN. Private Loftis is charged with desertion January 25, 1865.
48. Newton Loftis, age 18, enlisted December 1864, at Knoxville, TN. Private Loftis died in the service of his country March 8, 1865.
49. James F. Mace, age 18, enlisted November 1864, at Knoxville, TN.
50. Wyley Madison, age 22, enlisted October 1864, at Bulls Gap, TN. Private Madison was the company "cold cook."
51. William L. Man, age 20, enlisted March 1864, at Mitchell County, NC. Private Man is charged with desertion December 3, 1864.

52. Samuel McCall, age 26, enlisted April 1864, at Transylvania County, NC.
53. Wilson McKee, age 26, enlisted November 1864, at Knoxville, TN.
54. Wyley G. Moody, age 30, enlisted March 1864, at Mitchell County, NC. Private Moody is charge with desertion April 2, 1865.
55. John W. Moore, age 33, enlisted March 1865, at Knoxville, TN.
56. Samuel Moore, age 21, enlisted April 1864, at Transylvania County, NC. Private Moore is charged with desertion January 26, 1865.
57. William L. Nelson, age 43, enlisted March 1864, at Mitchell County, NC. Private Nelson died in the service of his country December 1, 1864, in a Confederate prisoner of war camp in Mitchell County, NC.
58. William Paly, age 30, enlisted September 1864, at Bulls Gap, TN.
59. Carson Parker, age 18, enlisted November 1864, at Mitchell County, NC.
60. Hynam H. Persell, age 18, enlisted October 1864, at Jonesboro, TN.
61. Drury W. Patterson, age 18, enlisted November 1864, at Knoxville, TN.
62. William Phillips, age 18, enlisted March 1865, at Knoxville, TN.
63. James M. Ray, age 36, enlisted March 1865, at Knoxville, TN.
64. James M. Riddle, age 19, enlisted March 1865, at Mitchell County, NC.
65. Wyley Roberts, age 25, enlisted March 1865, at Knoxville, TN.
66. Jabes B. Sloan, age 18, enlisted March 1864, at Mitchell County, NC.
67. Charles Street, age 18, enlisted March 1864, at Mitchell County, NC.
68. William H. Street, age 18, enlisted March 1864, at Mitchell County, NC.
69. Jeremiah M. Taylor, age 18, enlisted October 1864, at Bulls Gap, TN.
70. Eli Vaughn, age 18, enlisted August 1864, at Knoxville, TN.
71. Joseph Williams, age 20, enlisted October 1864, at Bulls Gap, TN. Private Williams is charged with desertion December 3, 1864.
72. John C. Wilson, age 29, enlisted September 1864, at Yancey County, NC.
73. William Wilson, age 27, enlisted September 1864, at Yancey County, NC.
74. James L. Wright, age 18, enlisted August 1864, at Knoxville, TN. Private Wright is charged with desertion September 27, 1864.

Co f

STAFF

1. Captain John C. Garlin, no age, enlistment date, or place of enlistment is given.
2. First Lieutenant Ephraim A. Davis, age_ , enlisted October 1864, at Knoxville, TN. Lieutenant Davis was appointed as First Lieutenant by General Stoneman to serve with the Thirteenth Tennessee Cavalry.
3. Second Lieutenant William M. Campbell, age _ , enlisted December 1864, at Knoxville, TN. Lieutenant Campbell was appointed by General Stoneman to his position.
4. First Sergeant Rubin Garland, age 27, enlisted June 1864, at Burnsville, NC.
5. Sergeant Columbus H. Adams, age 24, enlisted October 1864, at Knoxville, TN.
6. Sergeant Dennis Brannan, age 25, enlisted October 1864, at Calhoun, NC.
7. Sergeant Jesse Keller, age 22, enlisted July 1864, at Knoxville, TN.
8. Corporal Daniel M. Mathison, age 22, enlisted September 1864, at Taylorsville, NC.
9. Corporal William M. Rich, age 18, enlisted November 1864, at Knoxville, TN.
10. Corporal Isaac A. Johnson, age 18, enlisted October 1864, at Calhoun, NC.
11. Corporal Calvin Tucker, age 18, enlisted November 1864, at Knoxville, TN.
12. Musician Nathan Pate, age 18, enlisted July 1864, at Knoxville, TN.
13. Musician Henry H. Nichols, age 25, enlisted August 1864, at Wilksboro, NC.
14. Wagoner John Burl, age 20, enlisted October 1864, at Bulls Gap, TN.

PRIVATE SOLDIERS

1. Hayser Adams, age 26, enlisted August 1864, at Wilksboro, NC
2. Ziri Adams, age 20, enlisted October 1864, at Knoxville, TN. Private Adams died in the service of his country at the military hospital in Knoxville, TN, March 14, 1865.
3. Jefferson Bailey, age 20, enlisted July 1864, at Burnsville, NC. Private Bailey is charged with desertion November 5, 1864, at Sevierville, TN.
4. Stephen M. Bailey, age 39, enlisted June 1864, at Knoxville, TN.

5. George F. Banks, age 18, enlisted June 1864, at Danridge, TN. Private Banks is charged with desertion July 20, 1865.
6. Abraham Bennett, age 17, enlisted July 1864, at Knoxville, TN.
7. Amos Bennett, age 18, enlisted July 1864, at Knoxville, TN.
8. Baxter Bennett, age 28, enlisted June 1864, at Knoxville, TN.
9. Jeremiah Bennett, age 30, enlisted October 1864, at Bulls Gap, TN.
10. John Bennett, Jr., age 23, enlisted June 1864, at Knoxville, TN.
11. William Bennett, age 20, enlisted June 1864, at Knoxville, TN.
12. William Blackburn, age 18, enlisted July 1864, at Knoxville, TN.
13. James Blevins, age 18, enlisted November 1864, at Knoxville, TN.
14. George H. Brown, age 21, enlisted August 1864, at Wilksboro, NC. Private Brown was promoted to Sergeant, and later First Lieutenant of Company K, Third Mounted Infantry.
15. Archibald Burnett, age 30, enlisted June 1864, at Knoxville, TN.
16. Albert E. Carpenter, 49, enlisted October 1864, at Mitchell County, NC.
17. Jonathan Carpenter, 18, enlisted October 1864, at Mitchell County, NC.
18. James W. Chapel, age 18, enlisted November 1864, at Knoxville, TN. Private Chapel is charged with desertion on December 29, 1864, at Grassy Cove, TN.
19. Adolphus Clark, age 42, enlisted May 1864, at Mitchell County, NC. Private Clark is charged with desertion November 5, 1864, at Sevierville, TN.
20. Detroit Clark, age 20, enlisted October 1864, at Mitchell County, NC. Private Clark is charged with desertion on November 5, 1864, at Sevierville, TN.
21. Thade Clark, age 20, enlisted October 1864, at Mitchell County, NC. Private Clark is charged with desertion on November 5, 1864, at Sevierville, TN.
22. Benjamin Cook, age 18, enlisted November 1864, at Knoxville, TN. Private Cook is charged with desertion on March 10, 1865, at Knoxville, TN.
23. Albert S. Cooper, age 18, enlisted July 1864, at Knoxville, TN.
24. John G. Cooper, age 38, enlisted August 1864, at Knoxville, TN. Private Cooper is charged with desertion on December 24, at Grassy Cove, TN.
25. William A. Cooper, age 18, enlisted June 1864, at Knoxville, TN.
26. Peter F. Danner, age 19, enlisted September 1864, at Knoxville, TN. Private Danner is charged with desertion June 22, 1865, at Greeneville, TN.

27. George F. Doly, age 18, enlisted September 1864, at Knoxville, TN. Private Doly died in the service of his country on December 20, 1864, at Paint Rock, NC. Private Doly was killed by the Confederate Army.
28. James J. Dryman, age 18, enlisted August 1864, at Elizabethton, TN. Private Dryman is charged with desertion on June 16, 1865, at Greeneville, TN.
29. William Fitch, age 38, enlisted October 1864, at Knoxville, TN. Private Fitch was the Company cook.
30. Philip Gardiner, age 19, enlisted November 1864, at Knoxville, TN. Private Gardiner is charged with desertion on June 12, 1865, at Greeneville, TN.
31. John Garland, age 30, enlisted June 1864, at Childsville, NC.
32. John Gregg, age 18, enlisted November 1864, at Knoxville, TN.
33. Reuben R. Hall, no age, year of enlistment, or place of enlistment are given.
34. David Hampton, age 44, enlisted June 1864, at Jonesboro, TN. Private Hampton is charged with desertion December 29, 1864, at Grassy Cove, TN.
35. Joseph Y. Hayes, age 19, enlisted August 6, 1864, at Wilksboro, NC.
36. John Henton, age 24, enlisted October 1864, at Knoxville, TN.
37. James Howell, age 20, enlisted July 1864, at Knoxville, TN.
38. James Hughes, age 27, enlisted June 1864, at Burnsville, NC. Private Hughes is charged with desertion December 29, at Grassy Cove, TN.
39. Jesse Hendren, age 38, enlisted August 1864, at Wilksboro, NC. Private Hendren died in the service of his country on March 28, 1865, at Brabston Mills, TN, due to illness.
40. Rueben Jennings, age 21, enlisted August 1864, at Wilksboro, NC. Private Jennings died in the service of his country on December 22, 1864.No cause of death, or place of death is given.
41. Russell Kite, age 19, enlisted October 1864, at Knoxville, TN.
42. Abraham Masters, age 44, enlisted June 1864, at Burnsville, NC
43. D. McClurth. Other aspects of Private McClurth's records are not legible.
44. George F. McGlanny, age 22, enlisted November 1864, at Knoxville, TN.
45. William McInturf, age 29, enlisted March 1864, at Knoxville, TN.
46. Jessup Meshek, age 27, enlisted June 1864, at Burnsville, NC. Private Meshek is charged with desertion on December 29, 1864, at Grassy Cove, TN.

47. Lorenzo D. Michael, age 18, enlisted July 1864, at Knoxville, TN.
48. Abraham A. Michals, age 18, enlisted August 1864, at Wilksboro, NC.
49. Elkanah Miller, age 18, enlisted November 1864, at Knoxville, TN.
50. Hiram Miller, age 35, enlisted June 1864, at Knoxville, TN.
51. Timothy, Miller, age 38, enlisted July 1864, at Burnsville, NC.
52. Purvis Minton, age 20, enlisted 1864, at Knoxville, TN.
53. Elisha K. Nelson, age 22, enlisted August 1864, at Bulls Gap, TN.
    Private Nelson is charged with desertion March 15, 1865, at Knoxville,
    TN.
54. Galloway Patterson, age 18, enlisted October 1864, at Mitchell County,
    NC.
55. Moses Peterson, Jr., age 18, enlisted June 1864, at Burnsville, NC.
56. Moses Peterson, Sr., age 23, enlisted June 1864, at Knoxville, TN.(
    Note: These two men obviously are not related as father and son. If so,
    the Company clerk made an error concerning the father's age.)
57. Reuben Peterson, age 33. enlisted June 1864, at Knoxville, TN.
58. Samuel Peterson, age 20, enlisted June 1864, at Knoxville, TN.
59. Columbus Phillips, age 18, enlisted November 1864, at Knoxville, TN.
60. William Pierce, age 18, enlisted October 1864, at Mitchell County, NC.
61. Harvey Presnell, age 30, enlisted June 1864, at Knoxville, TN.
62. Adolphus Pritchard, age 18, enlisted October 1864, at Calhoun, NC.
    Private Pritchard is charged with desertion on November 5, 1864, at
    Sevierville, TN.
63. William Pritchard, October 1864, at Mitchell County, NC. Private
    Pritchard is charged with desertion on November 5, 1864, at Sevierville,
    TN.
64. Jacob Ray, age 44, enlisted October 1864, at Burnsville, NC
65. Lewis W. Sabashine, age 19, enlisted February 1865, at Watauga
    County, NC.
66. James C. Slewder, age 21, enlisted October 1864, at Knoxville, TN.
67. James H. Starit, age 18, enlisted November 1864, at Knoxville, TN.
68. Joseph S. Stewart, age 18, enlisted October 1864, at Knoxville, TN.
69. James I. Teague, age 18, enlisted October 1864, at Mitchell County, NC.
70. John A. Thompson, age 28, enlisted August 1864, at Wilksboro, NC.
    Private Thompson is charged with desertion on April 17, 1865, at Boone,
    NC.
71. John D. Tipton, age 30, enlisted June 1864, at Knoxville, TN.

72. Jonathan Tipton, age 38, enlisted June 1864, at Knoxville, TN. Private Tipton died in the service of his country on February 4, 1865, at Knoxville, TN due to illness.
73. Samuel Tipton, age 40, enlisted March 1864, at Burnsville, NC.
74. William Tipton, age 33, enlisted July 1864, at Knoxville, TN.
75. Lewis W. Triplett, age 18, enlisted October 1864, at Knoxville, TN.
76. Joseph M. Webb, age 26, enlisted October 1864, at Mitchell County, NC. Private Webb is charged with desertion on November 5, 1864, at Sevierville, TN.
77. William Williams, age 29, enlisted October 1864, at Bulls Gap, TN. Private Williams is charged with desertion on November 5, 1864, at Sevierville, TN.
78. Leoi Wilson, age 18, enlisted October 1864, at Knoxville, TN. Private Wilson is charged with desertion on July 1, 1865, at Greeneville, TN.
79. William G. Youngor, age 32, enlisted August 1864, at Wilksboro, NC.

Co g

STAFF

1. Captain William M. Moore, age 32, enlisted March 1865, at Knoxville, TN.
2. First Sergeant Abraham Carter, age 39, enlisted March 1864, at Knoxville, TN.
3. Sergeant Sanders Tipton, age 29, enlisted August 1864, at Knoxville, TN.
4. Sergeant Wily J. Worly, age 39, enlisted December 1864, at Burnsville, NC.
5. Sergeant James W. Young, age 20, enlisted October 1864, at Yancey County, NC.
6. Sergeant Aaron J. Burton, age 19, enlisted December 1864, at Burnsville, NC.
7. Corporal George W. Johnson, age 20, enlisted October 1864, at Knoxville, TN.
8. Corporal Elias Laughter, age 18, enlisted November 1864, at Knoxville, TN.
9. Corporal Thomas S. Edwards, age 18, enlisted February 1865, at Knoxville, TN.
10. Drummer James Rice, age 23, enlisted January 1865, at Burnsville, NC.
11. Fife player Thomas Kinsley, age 20, enlisted October 1864, at Bulls Gap, TN.

PRIVATE SOLDIERS

1. William Austin, age 25, enlisted October 1864, at __.
2. James R.Ballard, age 22, enlisted January 1865, at Knoxville, TN.
3. James P. Ballard, age 19, enlisted January 1865, at Knoxville, TN.
4. ___ Banks, age 18, enlisted February 1865, at Knoxville, TN.
5. __ Black, age 23, enlisted January 1865, at Knoxville, TN. Private Black is charged with desertion. No details are given.
6. James Brady, age 23, enlisted September 1864, at Bulls Gap, TN.
7. James Buckner, age 29, enlisted January 1865, at Burnsville, NC.
8. James Burleson, age 18, enlisted October 1864, at Yancey County, NC.
9. __ Burleson, age 18, enlisted February 1865, at Knoxville, TN. Private Burleson left the Regiment April 16, 1865. The reason for his departure is unclear.
10. George A. Coat, age 27, enlisted January 1865, at Knoxville, TN.

11. Corbin (?) Cody, age 19, enlisted December 1864, at Knoxville, TN.
12. William (?) Cody, age 23, enlisted December 1864, at Knoxville, TN.
13. Adolphos Cordell, age 22, enlisted January 1865, at Knoxville, TN.
14. Daniel Cordell, age 24, enlisted January 1865, at Knoxville, TN.
15. William Edwards, age 18, enlisted February 1865, at Knoxville, TN.
16. William Fender, age 25, enlisted October 1864, at Knoxville, TN.
17. Melvin Fox, age 18, enlisted February 1865, at Knoxville, TN.
18. _____ Garner, age 22, enlisted October 1864, at Knoxville, TN.
19. John Gasnell, age 19, enlisted June 1864, at Knoxville, TN.
20. Charles Gunter, age 39, enlisted September 1864, at Bulls Gap, TN.
21. Henry Hair, age 18, enlisted September 1864, at Knoxville, TN.
22. Levi Hall, age 23, enlisted October 1864, at Knoxville, TN.
23. Amos Hensley, age_ , enlisted October 1864, at __. Private Hensley received a Dishonorable Discharge March 8, 1865. The reason for this action is not given.
24. John H. Hensley, age 33, enlisted August 1864, at Knoxville, TN.
25. Matherson Hensley, age 32, enlisted March 1864, at Knoxville, TN.
26. ___ Hensly, age 18, enlisted September 1864, at Bulls Gap, TN.
27. ___ Hensly, age 29, enlisted July 1864, at Knoxville, TN.
28. ___ Hensly, age 18, enlisted June 1864, at Madison County, NC.
29. ___ Hensly, age 18, enlisted January 1865, at Knoxville, TN.
30. ___ Henson, age 40, enlisted 1864, at Bulls Gap, TN.
31. James H. Higgins, age 18, enlisted October 1864, at Knoxville, TN.
32. Eli Hinson, age 19, enlisted October 1864, at Yancey County, NC.
33. ___ Hull, age 18, enlisted October 1864, at Knoxville, TN.
34. John W. Lorance, age 26, enlisted October 1864, at Knoxville, TN.
35. John McCrackins, age 18, enlisted February 1865, at Knoxville, TN.
36. Daniel Mills, age 18, enlisted October 1864, at Bulls, Gap, TN.
37. John Mills, age 19, enlisted October 1864, at Bulls Gap, TN.
38. John Mitcalf, age, _____ , enlisted ___, at _____.
39. John Norton, age 18, enlisted September 1864, at Bulls Gap TN.
40. John Norwood, age 36, enlisted August 1864, at Newport, TN.
41. ____ Osburn, age 18, enlisted October 1864, at Knoxville, TN.
42. Charles Penland, age 18, enlisted October 1864, at Yancey County, NC.
43. Jesse Penland, age 18, enlisted October 1864, at Yancey County, NC.
44. Andrew Pinion, age 20, enlisted February 1865, at Knoxville, TN.
45. Isiah Price, age 44, enlisted September 1864, at Bulls Gap, TN.
46. Noah (?) Pruitt (?) , age 19, enlisted June 1864, at Knoxville, TN.
47. William Prysock, age 19, enlisted June 1864, at Knoxville, TN.

48. William S. Ray, age 19, enlisted June 1864, at Bulls Gap, TN.
49. Wesley Rico, age 19, enlisted June 1864, at Knoxville, TN.
50. Jasper Roggers, age 18, enlisted January 1864, at Knoxville, TN.
51. Andrew Shelton, age 18, enlisted March 1864, at Mitchell County, NC.
52. David Shelton, age 30, enlisted July 1864, at Burnsville, NC.
53. Elifus Shelton, age 19, enlisted May 1864, at Knoxville, TN.
54. James Shelton, age 36, enlisted June 1864, at Knoxville, TN.
55. Gion(?) Slines(?) , age 21, enlisted September 1864, at Bulls Gap, TN.
56. Peter Southerland, age 34, enlisted February 1865, at Knoxville, TN.
57. William Stills, age 18, enlisted September 1864, at Bulls Gap, TN.
58. Valentine Tipton, age 44, enlisted August 1864, at Knoxville, TN.
59. __ Walker, age 44, enlisted October 1864, at Knoxville, TN.
60. Isom Walker, age 18, enlisted October 1864, at Knoxville, TN.
61. Rufus Weaver, age 35, enlisted September 1864, at Bulls Gap, TN.
62. William Westbrook, age 18, enlisted December 1864, at Bulls Gap, TN.
63. Madison Whitson, age 18, enlisted February 1865, at Knoxville, TN.
64. Robert Williams, age 18, enlisted January 1864, at Knoxville, TN.
65. Edward Wilson, age ____, enlisted _____, at _____.

Co h

STAFF

1. Captain William B. Underwood, age 21, enlisted February 1865, at Knoxville, TN.
2. First Lieutenant Aaron Vancannen, age 33, enlisted February 1865, at Knoxville, TN.
3. Second Lieutenant William W. Hubbard, age 18, enlisted February 1865, at Knoxville, TN.
4. First Sergeant William Vancannon, age 24, enlisted January 1865, at Knoxville, TN.
5. Sergeant Aaron Wright, age 44, enlisted January 1865, at Knoxville, TN.
6. Sergeant William H. Davis, age 25, enlisted December 1864, at Knoxville, TN.
7. Sergeant Leander W. Hall, age 37, enlisted January 1865, at Knoxville, TN.
8. Sergeant John J. Jennings, age 31, enlisted January 1865, at Knoxville, TN.
9. First Corporal Christopher C. Hampton, age 32, enlisted November 1864, at Knoxville, TN.
10. Corporal Columbus F. Armstrong, age 37, enlisted December 1864, at Knoxville, TN.
11. Corporal Daniel D. Woodruff, age 40, enlisted January 1865, at Knoxville, TN.
12. Corporal Leander Muller, age 44, enlisted January 1865, at Knoxville, TN.
13. Corporal Isaac L. Collins, age 42, enlisted January 1865, at Knoxville, TN.
14. Musician Jesse F. Yates, age 19, enlisted December 1864, at Jonesboro, TN.

PRIVATE SOLDIERS

1. William H. Adams, age 34, enlisted January 1865, at Knoxville, TN. Adams was promoted to Corporal February 16, 1865. Corporal Adams is charged with desertion April 15, 1865, at Boone, NC.

2. Mines A. Arboy, age 35, enlisted January 1865, at Knoxville, TN. Arboy was promoted to Corporal on February 15, 1865. Corporal Arboy is charged with desertion on April 15, 1865, at Boone, NC.
3. Solomon Bangass, age 31, enlisted August 1864, at Knoxville, TN. Private Bangass is charged with desertion on April 15, 1825, at Boone, NC.
4. George Blackburn, age___ , enlisted June 1865, at Knoxville, TN. Private Blackburn is charged with desertion on April 15, 1865,at Boone, NC.
5. William Blackburn, age 44, enlisted January 1865, at Knoxville, TN.
6. Joseph Barches, age 18, enlisted February 1865, at Watauga County, NC. Private Barches is charged with desertion on April 15, 1865, at Boone, NC.
7. Aaron Brown, age 40, enlisted January 1865, at Knoxville, TN. Corporal Brown was discharged from the Knoxville General Hospital on July 13, 1865.
8. Mark Brown, age 19, enlisted January 1865, at Knoxville, TN. Private Brown died in the service of his country at Knoxville General Hospital on April 3, 1865.
9. Elbert J. Burgner, age 23, enlisted September 1864, at Jonesboro, TN.
10. Andrew C. Caldwell, age 18, enlisted January 1865, at Knoxville, TN.
11. David M. Caldwell, age 18, enlisted January 1865, at Knoxville, TN.
12. Hamilton Caldwell, age 22, enlisted January 1865, at Knoxville, TN. Private Caldwell is charged with desertion on April 2, 1865, at Jonesboro, TN.
13. James A. Caldwell, age 27, enlisted January 1865, at Knoxville, TN.
14. William Capps, age 23, enlisted January 1865, at Knoxville, TN. Private Capps was appointed Drum major and transferred to the Regimental Staff on March 14, 1865.
15. William Carter, age 38, enlisted October 1864, at Knoxville, TN. Private Carter died in the service of his country on May 21, 1865, at the Knoxville General Hospital
16. John Chandler, age 18, enlisted December 1864, at Knoxville, TN.
17. General G. W. Church, age 18, enlisted January 1865, at Knoxville, TN.
18. Jordan Church, age 30, enlisted January 1865, at Knoxville, TN. Church was promoted to Corporal on February 16, 1865. Corporal Church is charged with desertion on April 15, 1865, at Boone NC.
19. Richard M. Clark, age 22, enlisted October 1864, at Knoxville, TN.

20. John Clary, age 28, enlisted January 1865, at Knoxville, TN. Private Clary died in the service of his country on April 10, 1865, at the Knoxville General Hospital.
21. William Clary, age 35, enlisted January 1865, at Knoxville, TN.
22. John Clinton, age 30, enlisted November 1864, at Knoxville, TN. Private Clinton was transferred to Company A, Third Mounted Infantry on April 1, 1865. (Note Private Clinton also appears on Company A roster.)
23. Lund Cooper, age 18, enlisted January 1865, at Knoxville, TN.
24. William A. Correl, age _ , enlisted August 1864, at Knoxville, TN.
25. D.A. Criag, age 18, enlisted January 1865, at Knoxville, TN. Private Criag was discharged from the Knoxville General Hospital on May 15, 1865, for medical reasons.
26. Joseph Cross, age 18, enlisted January 1865, at Knoxville, TN.
27. William C. Dunbar, age 18, enlisted December 1864, at Knoxville, TN.
28. Herander Edington, age 19, enlisted January 1865, at Knoxville, TN.
29. John Eusly, age 28, enlisted January 1865, at Knoxville, TN.
30. Robert P. Fowler, age 28, enlisted December 1864, at Washington County, TN.
31. Charles Garland, age 18, enlisted February 1864, at Knoxville, TN.
32. William M. Gregory, age 18, enlisted December 1864, at Washington County, TN. Private Gregory is charged with desertion on April 2, 1865, at Jonesboro, TN.
33. George Hall, age 29, enlisted January 1865, at Knoxville, TN.
34. James Handy- all information on Private Handy is illegible.
35. Joel Handy, age 30, enlisted January 1865, at Knoxville, TN.
36. Thomas Hardy- all information on Private Hardy is illegible.
37. Joseph E. Harrison, age 19, enlisted February 1865, at Watauga, NC.
38. Charles Headrick, age 44, enlisted January 1865, at Knoxville, TN.
39. James Headrick, age 18, enlisted January 1865, at Knoxville, TN.
40. George Henderson, age 18, enlisted January 1865, at Knoxville, TN.
41. Stephen A. Hoft, age 18, enlisted January 1865, at Knoxville, TN.
42. John A. Johnson, age 19, enlisted February 1865, at Wilksboro, NC. Private Johnson is charged with desertion on April 12, 1865, at Boone, NC.
43. Samuel Kilby, age 27, enlisted January 1865, at Knoxville, TN. Private Kilby is charged with desertion on April 15, 1865, at Boone, NC.
44. William J. Kilby, age 18, enlisted January 1865, at Knoxville, TN.

45. Levi Lang, age 23, enlisted December 1864, at Knoxville, TN. Private Lang is charged with desertion on April 15, 1865, at Boone, NC.

46. Thady Lang, age 18, enlisted October 1864, at Knoxville, TN.

47. John E. Massey, age 34, enlisted January 1865, at Knoxville, TN.

48. Samuel Moore, age 37, enlisted October 1864, at Jonesboro, TN.

49. Benjamin Mosely, age 18, enlisted January 1865, at Knoxville, TN.

50. John Mosely, age 18, enlisted January 1865, at Knoxville, TN. Private Mosely died in the service of his country on April 10, 1865, at the Knoxville General Hospital.

51. John A. Palmer, age 27, enlisted January 1865, at Knoxville, TN. Private Palmer is charged with desertion on April 2, 1865, at Jonesboro, TN.

52. Hiram J. Penlen, age 18, enlisted January 1865, at Knoxville, TN.

53. Hugh Phillips, age 31, enlisted January 1865, at Knoxville, TN. Private Phillips is charged with desertion on April 17, 1865, at Boone, NC.

54. William Phillips, age 18, enlisted January 1865, at Knoxville, TN. Private Phillips is charged with desertion on April 17, 1865, at Boone, NC.

55. Joseph Ray, age 18, enlisted January 1865, at Knoxville, TN.

56. Thomas H. Revis, age 29, enlisted January 1865, at Knoxville, TN.

57. Benjamin A. Rhodes, age 30, enlisted November 1864, at Knoxville, TN. Private Rhodes is charged with desertion on January 19, 1865, at Greeneville, TN.

58. John A. Rhoads, age 22, enlisted January 1865, at Knoxville, TN.

59. William D. Rhoads, age 22, enlisted January 1865, at Knoxville, TN.

60. Moses Richardson, age 20, enlisted January 1865, at Knoxville, TN.

61. Euack C. Shumate, age 20, enlisted January 20, 1865, at Knoxville, TN.

62. Mark H. Shumate, age 21, enlisted January 1865, at Knoxville, TN. Private died in the service of his country on March 19, 1865, at the Knoxville General Hospital.

63. Wesley Shumate, age 22, enlisted January 1865, at Knoxville, TN.

64. William Sneede, age _ , enlisted November 1864, at Knoxville, TN.

65. Martin Stamy, age 30, enlisted January 1865, at Knoxville, TN.

66. Daniel Stout, age __ , enlisted January 1865, at Knoxville, TN.

67. Jacob Tapp, age 19, enlisted December 1864, at Knoxville, TN. Private Tapp was transferred to Company A, Third Mounted Infantry on April 1, 1865. (Note: Private Tapp will also appear on Company A roster.)

68. Vincent Tapp, age 25, enlisted December 1864, at Knoxville, TN. Private Tapp was transferred to Company A, Third Mounted Infantry on

April 1, 1865.(Note: Private Tapp will also appear on Company A roster.)

69. William A. Tnell, age _____ , enlisted December 1864, at Knoxville, TN.
70. Elbert G. Triplet, age __ , enlisted October 1864, at Wilksboro, NC.
71. John A. Walker, age 20, enlisted January 1865, at Knoxville, TN.
    Private Walker is charged with desertion on April 12, 1865,Boone, NC.
72. James W. Walker, age __ , enlisted January 1865, at Knoxville, TN.
73. Rolet Walker, age _____ , enlisted February 1865, at Wilksboro, NC
74. John A. Willis, age ___ , enlisted October 1864, at Burnsville, NC.
75. Silas Williams, age 18, enlisted February 1865, at Knoxville, TN.
    Private Williams is charged with desertion on June 19, 1865, at Greeneville, TN.
76. William M. Wood, age __ , enlisted February 1865, at North Wilksboro, NC.
77. John D. Yates, age 20, enlisted December 1864, at Jonesboro, TN.

Co I

STAFF

1. Captain Robert J. Morrison, age 25, enlisted March 1865, at Knoxville, TN.
2. First Lieutenant James Hartley, age 34, enlisted March 1865, at Knoxville, TN.
3. Second Lieutenant Cummings, age 28, enlisted March 1865, at Knoxville, TN.
4. First Sergeant Thomas Rice, age 31, enlisted February 1865, at Knoxville, TN.
5. Sergeant Hiram Ray, age 25, enlisted March 1865, at Knoxville, TN.
6. Sergeant George Shackleford, age 21, enlisted January 1865, at Knoxville, TN.
7. Sergeant William R, Inelson, age 25, enlisted January 1865, at Knoxville, TN.
8. Sergeant Finley Queen, age 25, enlisted January 1865, at Knoxville, TN.
9. Corporal Solomon D. Dellinger, age 21, enlisted March 1865, at Knoxville, TN.
10. Corporal Jonathan McPeters, age 26, enlisted March 1865, at Knoxville, TN.
11. Corporal Mason Gilreath (?), age 34, enlisted March 1865, at Knoxville, TN.
12. Corporal Solomon Whitaker, age 38, enlisted March 1865, at Knoxville, TN.
13. Corporal Harry M. Hampton, age 20, enlisted March 1865, at Knoxville, TN.
14. Corporal Bartlet Mullin, age 21, enlisted January 1865, at Knoxville, TN.
15. Corporal Robert K. Roberts, age 18, enlisted March 1865, at Knoxville, TN.
16. Musician James Wilborn, age 44, enlisted January 1865, at Knoxville, TN.
17. Musician James C, Rymer, age 24, enlisted March 1865, at Knoxville, TN.
18. Teamster William B. Horton, age 40, enlisted January 1865, at Knoxville, TN.

PRIVATE SOLDIERS

1. Nathan Allen, age 44, enlisted December 1864, at Knoxville, TN.
2. William Allen, age 18, enlisted March 1865, at Knoxville, TN.
3. Robert D. Arowood, age 29, enlisted January 1865, at Knoxville, TN.
4. William S. Bostick, age 28, enlisted March 1865, at Knoxville, TN.
5. John T. Bowens, age 30, enlisted January 1865, at Knoxville, TN.
6. William Bowens, age _____ , enlisted February 1865, at Knoxville, TN.
7. Samuel D. Byrd, age 18, enlisted March 1865, at Knoxville, TN. Private Byrd is charged with desertion on June 10, 1865, at Greeneville, TN.
8. William Byrd, age 24, enlisted January 1865, at Knoxville, TN.
9. James Campbell. All information on Private Campbell is illegible. Private Campbell is charged with desertion. The date of the offense is illegible, the place of desertion is Greeneville, TN.
10. Acey Chambers, age 27, enlisted March 1865, at Knoxville, TN.
11. Alfred Church, age 19, enlisted March 1865, at Knoxville, TN. Private Church is charged with desertion on March 1, 1865, at Carter County, TN.
12. John J. Church, age 30, enlisted January 1865, at Knoxville, TN. Private Church is charged with desertion on March 22, 1865, at Carter County, TN.
13. Silas C. Cilton, age 18, enlisted March 1865, at Knoxville, TN.
14. Kinsey Citton, age 18, enlisted January 1865, at Knoxville, TN. Private Citton is charged with desertion on March 26, 1865, at Greene County, TN.
15. William Cook, age 18, enlisted January 1865, at Knoxville, TN. Private Cook is charged with desertion on May 1, 1865, at Asheville, NC.
16. Morgan S. Darnell, age 18, enlisted February 1865, at Knoxville, TN.
17. Leander Dowell, age 25, enlisted January 1865, at Knoxville, TN.
18. Pickney Dowell, age 18, enlisted January 1865,at Knoxville, TN.
19. William A. Dowell, age 18, enlisted January 1865, at Knoxville, TN. Private Dowell died in the service of his country on March 26, 1865, at the Knoxville, General Hospital.
20. William L. Dowell, age 18, enlisted January 1865, at Knoxville, TN. Private Dowell died in the service of his country on March 28, 1865, at the Knoxville General Hospital.
21. John Eades, age 24, enlisted January 1865, at Knoxville, TN.
22. Francis Ealey, age 18, enlisted January 1865, at Knoxville, TN.
23. Allen Edwards, age 22, enlisted March 1865, at Knoxville, TN.

24. James Edwards, age 18, enlisted February 1865, at Knoxville, TN. Private Edwards is charged with desertion on May 1, 1865, at Asheville, NC.
25. Timothy Edwards, age 18, enlisted March 1865, at Knoxville, TN.
26. Thomas Edwards, age 38, enlisted March 1865, at Knoxville, TN.
27. Martin Fowler, age 18, enlisted March 1865, at Knoxville, TN.
28. Alfred Goforth, age 18, enlisted March 1865, at Knoxville, TN.
29. Hensley T. Henderson, age 18, enlisted February 1865, at Knoxville, TN.
30. Otto Hildbrand, age 19, enlisted March 1865, at Knoxville, TN. Private Hildbrand was promoted to Sergeant and transferred to the Regimental Headquarters.
31. Hastings A. Horton, age 27, enlisted January 1865, at Knoxville, TN. Private Horton died in the service of his country on January 5, 1865, at the Knoxville General Hospital. Private Horton's death occurred four days after his enlistment.
32. William R. Horton, age 18, enlisted March 1865, at Knoxville, TN. Private Horton was the Company Cold Cook.
33. Francis Jinkens, age 38, enlisted March 1865, at Knoxville, TN. Private Jinkens is charged with desertion on May 1, 1865, at Asheville, NC.
34. Richard Kerly, age 42, enlisted March 1865, at Knoxville, TN.
35. William Lambreath, age 31, enlisted February 1865, at Knoxville, TN.
36. William C. Lamissing, age 26, enlisted October 1864(?), at Knoxville, TN. Private Lamissing transferred to Company F, Second Mounted Infrantry, North Carolina Vols.
37. John M. Laws, age 23, enlisted January 1865, at Knoxville, TN. Private Laws is charged with desertion on March 27, 1865, at Washington County, TN.
38. Thomas Mahalffey, age 19, enlisted February 1865, at Knoxville, TN. Private Mahalffey died in the service of his country on April 20, 1865, in the Knoxville General Hospital.
39. William Marlow, age 18, enlisted March 1865, at Knoxville, TN.
40. James Mason, age 18, enlisted February 1865, at Knoxville, TN. Private Mason died in the service of his Country on May 18, 1865, at the Knoxville General Hospital.
41. Rufus T. McClain, age 41, enlisted March 1865, at Knoxville, TN. Private McClain was discharged for medical reasons on June 24, 1865.
42. Samuel McClure, age 28, enlisted September 1864, at Bulls Gap, TN. Private McClure was the Company Cold Cook.

43. Samuel McKinney, age 18, enlisted March 1865, at Knoxville, TN.

44. James Medley, age 18, enlisted February 1865, at Knoxville, TN.

45. Ruben Medlock, age 35, enlisted February 1865, at Knoxville, TN. Private Medlock died in the service of his country on April 1, 1865, at Knoxville General Hospital.

46. G. Michael, age 18, enlisted March 1865, at Knoxville, TN.

47. William Midcalf, age 18, enlisted February 1865, at Knoxville, TN. Private Midcalf is charged with desertion on July 3, 1865, at Greeneville, TN.

48. Jesse M. Miller, age 20, enlisted January 1865, at Knoxville, TN.

49. Marcus Miller, age 18, enlisted January 1865, at Knoxville, TN.

50. William Moore, age 18, enlisted March 1865, at Knoxville, TN. Private Moore is charged with desertion on July 15, 1865, at Greeneville, TN.

51. Joseph T. Norton, age 23, enlisted January 1865, at Knoxville, TN.

52. Joseph Pardue, age 18, enlisted February 1865, at Knoxville, TN.

53. Isedell Privatt, age 20, enlisted January 1865, at Knoxville, TN.

54. Millas T. Privatt, age 19, enlisted January 1865, at Knoxville, TN.

55. Pickney Queen, age 18, enlisted January 1865, at Knoxville, TN. Private Queen died in the service of his country on April 12, 1865, at Knoxville General Hospital.

56. Samuel R. Queen, age 19, enlisted January 1865, at Knoxville, TN.

57. William R. Queen, age 19, enlisted January 1865, at Knoxville, TN.

58. Nathan W. Rains, age 21, enlisted March 1865, at Knoxville, TN.

59. James Reece, age 18, enlisted February 1865, at Knoxville, TN.

60. Augustus Reed, age 18, enlisted January 1865, at Knoxville, TN.

61. James Robbins, age 18, enlisted March 1865, at Knoxville, TN. Private Robbins was promoted to Sergeant and transferred to the Company Staff on June 14, 1865.

62. Calvin D. Santon, age 25, enlisted March 1865, at Knoxville, TN.

63. David Saylor, age 18, enlisted February 1865, at Knoxville, TN.

64. David W. Seacey, age 27, enlisted October 1864, at Knoxville, TN.

65. James M. Seay, age 24, enlisted February 1865, at Knoxville, TN.

66. Elijah Sercey, age 19, enlisted October 1864, at Knoxville, TN. Private Sercey died in the service of his country on April 25, 1865, at the Knoxville General Hospital.

67. John T. Spaun (?), age 24, enlisted March 1865, at Knoxville, TN.

68. William Spigner, age 22, enlisted January 1865, at Knoxville, TN.

69. Thomas Stacey, age 21, enlisted January 1865, at Knoxville, TN.

70. Melvin M. Steward, 23, enlisted December 1864, at Knoxville, TN.

71. Murphy Stout, age 18, enlisted January 1865, at Knoxville, TN. Private Stout is charged with desertion on March 26, 1865, at Washington County, TN.
72. Jonathan Sullivan, age 18, enlisted March 1865, at Knoxville, TN. Private Sullivan is charged with desertion on June 12, 1865, at Greeneville, TN.
73. Robert Templeton, age 18, enlisted February 1865, at Knoxville, TN.
74. William Walker, age 18, enlisted March 1865, at Knoxville, TN. Private Walker died in the service of his country on July 26, 1865, at the Knoxville General Hospital.
75. Samuel Wallace, age 40, enlisted January 1865, at Knoxville, TN.
76. William Wallace, age 23, enlisted January 1865, at Knoxville, TN.
77. Albert West, age 18, enlisted March 1865, at Knoxville, TN.
78. Ambrous White, age 23, enlisted January 1865, at Knoxville, TN.
79. Leander Wilborn, age 21, enlisted January 1865, at Knoxville, TN.
80. Thomas Wilborn, age 22, enlisted January 1865, at Knoxville, TN.
81. Manteville Wright, age 27, enlisted March 1865, at Knoxville, TN.
82. Joseph Younger, age 26, enlisted March 1865, at Knoxville, TN. Private Younger was promoted to Corporal March 14, 1865. Corporal Younger died in the service of his country July 15, 1865, at the Knoxville General Hospital.

Cok

STAFF

1. Captain John Ray, enlisted March 1865, at Knoxville, TN.
2. First Lieutenant George H. Brown, enlisted March 1865, at Knoxville, TN.
3. Second Lieutenant John G. Wilson, enlisted March 1865, at Knoxville, TN.
4. First Sergeant Henry Howard, enlisted March 1865, at Burnsville, NC.
5. Sergeant Tilman H. McCuray, enlisted March 1865, at Burnsville, NC.
6. Sergeant William K. Chambers. enlisted March 1865, at Burnsville, NC.
7. Sergeant Amos Boon, enlisted March 1865, at Burnsville, NC.
8. Sergeant William B. Biggs, enlisted March 1865, at Burnsville, NC.
9. Corporal Jephaniah McCuray, enlisted March 1865, at Burnsville, NC.
10. Corporal James Biggs, enlisted March 1865, at Burnsville, NC.
11. Corporal Joseph B. Chambers, enlisted March 1865, at Burnsville, NC.
12. Corporal James K. Buckner, enlisted March 1865, at Burnsville, TN.
13. Corporal Jacob A. Phipps, enlisted March 1865, at Burnsville, NC.
14. Corporal John Riddle, enlisted March 1865, at Burnsville, NC.
15. Corporal John Carter, enlisted March 1865, at Burnsville, NC.
16. Corporal William Ray, enlisted March 1865, at Burnsville, NC.
17. Musician Adolphus Hensley, enlisted March 1865, at Burnsville, NC.
18. Musician Thomas E. Ray, enlisted March 1865, at Burnsville, NC.
19. Wagoner Goodson M. Hensley, enlisted March 1865, at Burnsville, NC.

PRIVATE SOLDIERS

1. Adensuim D. Allen, enlisted March 1865, at Burnsville, NC.
2. Young Allen, enlisted March 1865, at Burnsville, NC.
3. William F. Andens, enlisted March 1865, at Burnsville, NC.
4. Hiram J. Anders, enlisted March 1865, at Burnsville, NC.
5. Andrew Austin, enlisted March 1865, at Burnsville, NC.
6. Clingman L. Austin, enlisted March 1865, at Burnsville, NC.
7. William B. Banks, enlisted March 1865, at Burnsville, NC. Private Banks left the Regiment on April 25, 1865, due to illness. Private Banks was hospitalized in Greene County, TN Hospital.
8. Hezekiak K. Brooks, enlisted March 1864, at Burnsville, NC.
9. Levi Buckner, enlisted March 1865, at Burnsville, NC.
10. William Carter, enlisted March 1865, at Burnsville, NC.
11. Henry Crawford, enlisted March 1865, at Burnsville, NC.

12. John Dodd, enlisted March 1865, at Burnsville, NC.

13. Zachanah Done, enlisted March 1865, at Burnsville, NC.

14. Morgan Done, enlisted March 1865, at Burnsville, NC.

15. Samuel Estep, enlisted March 1865, at Burnsville, NC.

16. Thomas J. Gardner, enlisted March 1865, at Burnsville, NC.

17. Lewis Gentry, enlisted March 1865, at Burnsville, NC.

18. Elbert Gillis, enlisted March 1865, at Burnsville, NC. Private Gillis was charged with desertion. The charge was later dismissed.

19. John Gregory, enlisted March 1865, at Burnsville, NC.

20. Milas Gregory, enlisted March 1865, at Burnsville, NC.

21. John W. Guthrie, enlisted March 1865, at Burnsville, NC.

22. Thaddeus Guthrie, enlisted March 1865, at Burnsville, NC.

23. Charles W. Hensley, enlisted March 1865, at Burnsville, NC.

24. Silas B. Hensley, enlisted March 1865, at Burnsville, NC. Private Hensley was reduced in rank from Sergeant to private for desertion on June 12, 1865.

25. William K. Hensley, enlisted March 1865, at Burnsville, NC.

26. John Holcombe, enlisted March 1865, at Burnsville, NC. Private Holcombe was charged with desertion. The charge was later withdrawn.

27. Mathew A. Lewis, enlisted March 1865, at Burnsville, NC.

28. James McLeumy, enlisted March 1865, at Burnsville, NC.

29. James O. McLeumy, enlisted March 1865, at Burnsville, NC.

30. Levi Mitcalf, enlisted March 1865, at Burnsville, NC.

31. James Morgan, enlisted March 1865, at Burnsville, NC. Private Morgan is charged with desertion. Private Morgan returned to duty under the President's Proclamation of Pardon. The charge was withdrawn.

32. James Morrow, enlisted March 1865, at Burnsville, NC,

33. William Mois (?), enlisted March 1865, at Burnsville, NC.

34. William Pigles, enlisted March 1865, at Burnsville, NC.

35. George W. Pigles, enlisted March 1865, at Burnsville, NC.

36. Barnett Ray, enlisted March 1865, at Burnsville, NC.

37. James W. Ray, enlisted March 1865, at Burnsville, NC.

38. Nathan W. Ray, enlisted March 1865, at Burnsville, NC.

39. Samuel B. Ray, enlisted March 1865, at Burnsville, NC.

40. Thomas J. Rinnion, enlisted March 1865, at Burnsville, NC.

41. William Riddle, enlisted March 1865, at Burnsville, NC.

NOTE: Company K has twelve men with illegible names, and identification information. This company is the most unusual of the Regiment's ten companies. All soldiers in this company enlisted in March 1865, at Burnsville, NC, except for the three officers. The age of the soldiers, at the time of enlistment, was not given by the Company K clerk.

End notes

ENDNOTES

1. Formation and Analysis of the Third Mounted Infantry, page 1.

i Fisher, Noel C. *War at Every Door: Partisan Politics & Guerrilla Violence in East Tennessee, 1860-1869*, p. 87. Hereinafter cited as Fisher.

ii Dyer, Frederick H., *A Compendium of the War of the Rebellion*, Vol. II, p. 1472. Hereinafter cited as Dyer's.

iii Current, Richard N., *Lincoln's Loyalists: Union Soldiers From the Confederacy*, p. 71. Hereinafter cited as Current.

iv *Official Records*, Vol. LII/ 1, p. 515. Hereinafter cited as OR.

v National Archives: *Official Mustering Out Records for the North Carolina Third Mounted Infantry Volunteers*. Hereinafter cited as Mustering Records.

vi Van Noppen, Ina W., *Stoneman's Last Raid*, p. 40. Hereinafter cited as van Noppen.

vii Mustering Records.

viii *Ibid.*

ix *Ibid.*

x *Ibid.*

xi Fox, William F., *Regimental Losses in the American Civil War: 1861-65*, p. 295. Hereinafter cited as Fox.

xii Mustering Records.

2.   Camp Vance Raid, page 4.

xiii *Official Army Register of Volunteer Forces of the United States Army, For the Years 1861-1865,* Part IV (West Virginia, Virginia, North Carolina, South Carolina, Georgia, Florida, Alabama, Mississippi, Louisiana, Texas, Arkansas, Tennessee, Kentucky), p. 1148. Hereinafter cited as Army Register.

xiv Barrett, John G., *The Civil War in North Carolina,* p. 233. Hereinafter cited as Barrett.

xv Crow, Vernon H., *Storm in the Mountains,* p. 105. Hereinafter cited as Crow; Trotter, William R., *Bushwhackers! The Civil War in North Carolina, The Mountains,* p. 116. Hereinafter cited as Trotter; Arthur, John P., *A History of Watauga County,* p. 164. Hereinafter as Arthur, Watauga County.

xvi *Ibid.*

xvii Arthur, *Watauga County,* p.164.

xviii *Ibid.*

xix Crow, p. 105.

xx Crow, p. 105; Phifer, Edward W., *Burke: History of a North Carolina County,* p. 325. Hereinafter cited as Phifer.

xxi Trotter, pg. 116-117; Phifer, p. 325.

xxii Arthur, *Watauga County,* p. 162.

xxiii Trotter, p. 116; Crow, p. 105; Arthur, *Watauga County,* p. 162.

xxiv *Official Records,* Vol. XXXIX/ 1, p. 225.

xxv *Ibid,* p. 236.

xxvi Crow, p. 106; Phifer, p.325.

xxvi Trotter, p. 118.

xxviii Crow, p. 106; Trotter, p. 118.

xxix Crow, p. 106; Phifer, p. 326; Arthur, *Watauga County,* p. 165.

xxx Crow, p. 106.

xxxi Trotter, p. 119.

xxxii *Official Records*, Vol. XXXIX/ 1, p. 234.

xxxiii *Ibid.,* p. 232,

xxxiv Fisher, p. 87.

xxxv *Ibid.*

xxxvi *Official Records,* Vol. XLV/ 1, p. 841.

3. Action at Morristown, Russellville, Big Pigeon, and Paint Rock, page 8.

xxxvii *Official Records, Vol. XXXIX,* / 1, p. 852.

xxxviii *Ibid.*

xxxix *Ibid.,* p. 854.

xl *Ibid.*

xli *Ibid.*

xlii *Ibid.*

xliii *Ibid.,* p. 851.

xliv *Ibid.*, p. 845-846.

xlv *Ibid.*, p. 846.

xlvi *Ibid.*

xlvii Warner, Ezra J., *Generals in Blue,* p. 289. Hereinafter cited as Warner;
    Trotter, p. 128; Sifakis, Stewart, *Who Was Who in the Confederacy,* p.
    289.

xlviii Dyer's, Vol. I, p. 874.

xlix *Ibid.*, p. 738.

l Ramage, James A., *Rebel Raider. The Life of John Hunt Morgan,* p.243.

li National Archives, *Surgeons Report,* Vol. 4, Main Western Theater,
    Section M- Tennessee.

lii *Official Records,* Vol. XLV/1 p. 811.

liii *Ibid.*, p. 812.

liv *Ibid.,* p. 813.

lv *Ibid.*, p. 842.

lvi *Ibid.*

ENDNOTES

4.   Raid on Waynesville, page 12.

lvii Barrett, p. 350 n; Crow, p. 121.
lviii Crow, p. 121; Trotter, p. 237.
lix Trotter, 237-239; Barrett, p. 350n; Crow, p. 123.
lx Crow, p. 123.

ENDNOTES

5. Stoneman's Raid, page 14.

lxi Dictionary of American Biography, "George Stoneman," Vol. IX, part 2, p.92.

lxii Van Noppen, p. 4.

lxiii *Official Records,* XLIX/ 1, p. 325; van Noppen, p. 4.

lxiv van Noppen, p. 11.

lxv *Official Records,* Vol. XLIX/1, p. 325-326.

lxvi Hartley, Chris J., "George Stoneman's 1865 Cavalry Raid," *Civil War Regiments: A Journal of the American War,* Vol. 6, no. 1, 1998, p. 74-92,p. 76. Hereinafter cited as Hartley.

lxvii Van Horn, Thomas B., *Army of the Cumberland,* p. 584. Hereinafter cited as Van Horn.

lxviii *Official Records,* Vol. XLIX/1, p. 338-339.

lxix Hartley, p. 76.

lxx Hartley, p. 79; Van Horn, p. 548.

lxxi Van Horn, 548; Anderson, John H., Mrs., " last Days of the Confederacy in North Carolina," *Confederate Veteran,* Vol. XXXIX, 1931, p. 20-23.p.23.

lxxii Arthur, John P., *Western North Carolina: A History from 1730 to 1913,*p. 157. Hereinafter cited as Arthur, Western North Carolina.

lxxiii Arthur, Western North Carolina, p. 231; van Noppen, p. 20.

lxxiv van Noppen, p. 21.

lxxv *Ibid.*

lxxvi *Ibid.,* p. 23.

lxxvii *Ibid.*

lxxviii *Official Records,* Vol. XLIX/ 1, p. 337; Hartley, p.81.

lxxix *Ibid.*

lxxx Van Horn, p. 549.

lxxxi *Ibid.,*p. 550.

lxxxii *Ibid.,*p. 551.

lxxxiii *Ibid.,* p. 551 and 324.

lxxxiv *Ibid.,*p. 339.

lxxxv *Ibid.*

ENDNOTES

6. Asheville: Western North Carolina Citadel
Waynesville and Franklin: the Last Raid, page 19.

lxxxvi Arthur, Western North Carolina, p. 619; Trotter, p. 291; Sondley, p. 691.
lxxxvii Barrett, p. 363.
lxxxviii *Ibid.*, 364.
lxxxix *Ibid.*; Ray, James M., "Asheville in 1865," *The Lyceum*, Vol. 1, no.4, p.5-7.
xc Crow, p. 130.
xci *Official Records,* Vol. XLIX/1, p. 31.
xcii *Ibid.*
xciii Sondley, p. 698.
xciv "Asheville, North Carolina," *The Confederate Veteran,* Vol. VI, 1898, p. 6.
xcv Sondley, p. 698.
xcvi Army Register, p. 1148.
xcvii Trotter, p. 297-300; Barrett, p. 391-2.
xcviii Barrett, p. 391.
xcix *Official Records,* Vol. XLIX/1, p. 339.

ENDNOTES

7. Brief Biography of George W. Kirk, page 26.

c 1850 Census of Greene County, Tennessee

ci *Ibid.*

cii *Ibid.*

ciii Current, p. 71.

civ Pension File, no. 286.39, Department of the Interior, Bureau of Pensions, October 11, 1895.

cv *Ibid.*

cvi Pension File, no. 286.39, October 23, 1895.

cvii *Ibid.*

cviii *Ibid.*

cix *Dictionary of North Carolina Biography*, Vol. 3, edited by William S. Powell, p. 369-370.

cx Hamilton, J.G., *Reconstruction in North Carolina,* p. 496-533.

cxi *Ibid.*

cxii Washington, DC City Directory, from 1861-1950. (Supplied by the District of Columbia Public Library)

cxiii Gilroy, California *Advocate*, February 18, 1905.

The bibliographical source listing contains some works not actually cited in the endnotes. An example is the etchings of Edwin Forbes. Also, some reference works are not cited in the endnotes but are viewed as essential to the research of this history. William Powell's *The North Carolina Gazetteer,* is an example. While not cited, this source served as a guide to many of the battle areas not normally visited by the average history buff. Some of the battle areas no longer exist on official state maps. Hence, a source such as Dr. Powell's is essential.

The outstanding portrait of the mounted infantryman immediately after the title page is not cited. This is the work of Dr. Christine Davis, staff member of the South Carolina Governor's School for the Arts, in Greenville, South Carolina. Dr. Davis was gracious enough to complete this work for inclusion in this history.

Map work was a personal, and difficult aspect of the source material. The maps used are for general reference only. In no way are the maps to be considered drawn to scale.

Photographs used in this work are all the product of personal work over the years. Some are of lesser quality than others. It is felt that the readers of this work might have a better understanding of the scope of the history of the Third Mounted Infantry with some photographic reference. The photograph of the Second and or Third Mounted Infantry encamped in Asheville, NC, is owned(the image) by the University of North Carolina. It is part of the North Carolina Collection. The University gave permission for a one time use of this image. The University holds the copyright of this image.

Anderson, John H., Mrs., "Last Days of the Confederacy in North Carolina", *Confederate Veteran,* Vol. XXXIX, 1931, 20-23.

Arthur, John P. *History of Watauga County,* Everett Waddey, Richmond, 1915.

Arthur, John P. *Western North Carolina: A History from 1730 to 1913,* Raleigh, 1914.

Asheville *Citizen Times,* July 17, 1960, photograph of Federal Troops, Second or Third North Carolina Mounted Infantry Volunteers, in Asheville, Spring, 1865, (written commentary only).

Barrett, John G., and Yearns, W. Buck, *North Carolina Civil War Documentary,* University of North Carolina Press, Chapel Hill, 1980.

Barrett, John G., *The Civil War in North Carolina,* University of North Carolina Press, Chapel Hill, 1963.

Confederate Veteran, "Asheville, North Carolina.", Broadfoot Publishing Company, Wilmington, 1988, Vol. V1, January-December, 1898.

Census Records, Greene County, Tennessee, 1850.

Crow, Vernon H., *Storm in the Mountains,* Museum of the Cherokee Indian, Cherokee, North Carolina, 1982.

Current, Richard N., *Lincoln's Loyalists: Union Soldiers from the Confederacy,* Oxford University Press, New York, 1992.

Dictionary of American Biography, Vol. IX, part 2, p. 92, "George Stoneman", Charles Scribner's Sons, New York, 1936.

Dictionary of North Carolina Biography, Vol. 3, edited by William S. Powell, University of North Carolina Press, Chapel Hill, 1988.

Dyer, Frederick H., *A Compendium of the War of the Rebellion,* Vol. I, Morningside Press, Dayton, Ohio, 1994.

Dyer, Frederick, H., *A Compendium of the War of the Rebellion,* Vol. II, Morningside Press, Dayton, Ohio, 1994.

Fisher, Noel C., *War at Every Door: Partisan Politics & Guerrilla Violence in East Tennessee, 1860-1869,* University of North Carolina Press, Chapel Hill, 1997.

Forbes, Edwin, *Civil War Etchings,* edited by William F. Dawson, Dover Publications, Mineola, New York, 1994.

Fox, William F., *Regimental Losses in The American Civil War: 1861-65,* Morningside Book Shop Press, Dayton, Ohio, 1985.

Gilroy, California *Advocate,* February 18, 1905.

Hamilton, J.G., *Reconstruction in North Carolina,* Peter Smith, Glouster, 1964.

Hartley, Chris J., "George Stoneman's 1865 Cavalry Raid." *Civil War Regiments: A Journal of the American Civil War,* Vol. 6, No.1, 1998, 74-92.

Hill, Daniel H., *Confederate Military History: North Carolina,* Vol. 5, Broadfoot Publishing Company, Wilmington, 1987.

National Archives Records, Main Western Theater, Section M- Tennessee, Skirmishes, November 5 and 6, 1864, report of Dr. Marion Roberts, Surgeon, North Carolina Third Mounted Infantry(U.S.).

North Carolina Collection, photograph of the Second and/or the Third North Carolina Mounted Infantry Volunteers, encamped at Asheville, NC, Spring of 1865, University of North Carolina. Used with permission .

Official Army Register of the Volunteer Forces of the United States Army, For the Years 1861-1865, Part 1V (West Virginia, Virginia, North Carolina, South Carolina, Georgia, Florida, Alabama, Mississippi, Louisiana, Texas, Arkansas, Tennessee, Kentucky), Adjutant General's Office, 1865, p. 1148.

Official Records, The War of the Rebellion, Vols. XXX1X, /1, 232,234, 235, 236; XLV/1, 841; XXXIX /1, 845-46, 851, 852, 854; XLIX/1, 31, 324, 325,326, 337, 338-39.

Phifer, Edward, W., *Burke: History of a North Carolina County,* Privately Printed, Morganton, North Carolina, 1977.

Powell, William S., *The North Carolina Gazetteer, A Dictionary of Tar Heel Places,* University of North Carolina Press, Chapel Hill, North Carolina, 1968.

Ramage, James A., *Rebel Raider: The Life of John Hunt Morgan,* University of Kentucky Press, Lexington, 1986.

Ray, James M., "Asheville in 1865," *The Lyceum,* Vol. 1, No. 4, 1890, 5-7.

Sifakis, Stewart, *Who Was Who in the Confederacy,* Facts on File, New York, 1988.

Sondley, F. A., *A History of Buncombe County North Carolina,* Reprint Company Publishers, Spartanburg, South Carolina, 1977.

Trotter, William R., *Bushwhackers! The Civil War In North Carolina, the Mountains,* John F. Blair Publisher, Winston Salem, 1988.

Van Horn, Thomas B., *Army of the Cumberland,* Konecky and Konecky, New York, 1875.

Van Noppen, Ina W., *Stoneman's Last Raid,* North Carolina State University Print Shop, Raleigh, 1966.

Warner, Ezra J., *Generals In Blue: Lives of the Union Commanders,* Louisiana State University Press, Baton Rouge, 1964.

Washington DC City Directory: 1861-1950, (Supplied by the District of Columbia Public Library).

www.ingramcontent.com/pod-product-compliance
Lightning Source LLC
LaVergne TN
LVHW021612080426
835510LV00019B/2536